The Canadian Dream

OrangeBooks Publication

1st Floor, Rajhans Arcade, Mall Road, Kohka, Bhilai, Chhattisgarh 490020

Website: **www.orangebooks.in**

First Edition, 2025

ISBN: 978-93-6554-579-1

Price: Rs. 299.00

Printed in India

THE CANADIAN DREAM

How Students, Professionals & Entrepreneurs Can Navigate Immigration, Find Opportunities & Build Wealth in Canada

DR. SWAPNIL KALE

OrangeBooks Publication
www.orangebooks.in

About the Author

[A Journey from Aspiration to Inspiration]

Imagine standing at the edge of a life-changing decision, filled with hope, a journey of challenges, ambition, and the dream of a better future. For many immigrants, this is where the journey begins: an aspiration to start anew in a land full of opportunities. For Dr. Swapnil Kale, the story wasn't just about personal triumph; it became a mission to help others navigate the same treacherous paths that once held him back. His life's work, embodied through *The Canadian Dream* and his pioneering consultancy, Migrant Master, stands as a beacon of hope for students, professionals, and entrepreneurs determined to build a new life in Canada.

The year was 2010, and like many ambitious individuals worldwide, Dr. Kale dreamed of building a better life in Canada, a country renowned for its inclusivity, booming economy, and opportunities for growth. However, what started as an exciting adventure soon turned into a harsh lesson. The immigration industry, shrouded in complexities and marred by fraudulent promises, became his first real challenge.

Dr. Kale was misled under the guise of the Express Entry points-based system. His file had been handled by a well-known immigration brand in India. However, due to a serious error on their part, the application was ultimately rejected by IRCC. The rejection came as a shock. When he contacted the agency for answers, he was stunned to learn that they lacked even a basic understanding of the proper documentation and processes. It was at that moment Dr. Kale realized there was a glaring disconnect between the requirements set by IRCC and what many consultants in the Indian market were actually practicing.

After falling prey to misleading consultants and losing significant financial resources to dishonest immigration firms, Dr. Kale came in a conclusion that the journey to Canada was not as transparent as it appeared. Instead of succumbing to defeat, he decided to take control of his destiny. His setbacks didn't just fuel his determination; they lit a fire that would transform him into a champion for others on similar paths.

Driven by his own experiences, Dr. Kale immersed himself in the intricacies of Canadian immigration law. He connected with RCIC-certified immigration lawyers, travelled extensively to gain firsthand knowledge of Canadian Permanent Residency (PR) processes, and learned the nuances of legal pathways that most applicants struggle to understand.

By 2011, his vision had crystallized. He founded Migrant Master, a consultancy dedicated to offering ethical, transparent, and expert immigration services. His goal was simple but profound: help people navigate the labyrinth of immigration laws without falling victim to scams, false promises, or bureaucratic pitfalls.

Over the past 14 years, Migrant Master has helped more than 6,000 families, 4,800 entrepreneurs, 3,500 working professionals, and over 12,000 students successfully migrate to Canada, the UK, the USA, and other parts of Europe. Today, it stands as a beacon of hope for immigrants worldwide who seek reliable, scam-free pathways to their Canadian dreams.

Through Migrant Master and his book, *The Canadian Dream*, Dr. Kale continues to change lives, one successful migration story at a time. His message is clear: "No dream is too big, and no challenge is too great, especially when you have the right guidance by your side."

So, whether you're a student ready to take the next big step, a professional seeking a fresh start, or an entrepreneur with global ambitions, know that with Dr. Swapnil Kale's expertise, the Canadian Dream isn't just possible; it's within your reach. The purpose of this book is not merely to share stories but to offer a correct approach and a practical solution to the ongoing issues within the immigration industry.

The Canadian Dream isn't just another immigration guide; it's an embodiment of Dr. Kale's mission.

Why Did I Write This Book?

When I set out on my own journey to Canada, I was filled with excitement, ambition, and a vision of a brighter future. Like many students, professionals, and entrepreneurs around the world, I believed that Canada was the perfect place to build a new life, one filled with opportunity, growth, and success.

But what I didn't expect were the challenges, roadblocks, and outright scams that stood in my way. I was misled by so-called "trusted" immigrati on consultants twice. I lost money, I lost time, I lost opportunities, and I lost confidence in the system. One such opportunity was a UK Highly Skilled Migrant Permit that I had already secured. However, based on a strong commitment from an immigration consultancy that I would be migrating to Canada within the next six months, I gave up that opportunity and returned to India. That decision, driven by false assurances, not only cost me a global opportunity but also deeply shook my faith in the immigration system itself.

Whether you're a student, a working professional, or an entrepreneur, I want you to have the information, strategies, and tools you need to succeed without falling into the traps that I once did.

The immigration industry, I realized, was filled with false promises, misinformation, and a lack of genuine guidance. Too many people were being exploited. Too many dreams were being crushed before they even had a chance to take off.

I refused to accept this as the norm.

I decided that if I couldn't find someone to guide me with honesty and transparency, I would become that guide for others.

Why Should You Read This Book?

Every year, thousands of students, professionals, and entrepreneurs dream of moving to Canada, the land of opportunity, stability, equality and prosperity. Yet, for many, this journey is filled with confusion, misinformation, and overwhelming challenges.

What if you had a clear, proven roadmap to help you navigate the process successfully?

That's exactly what this book offers.

The Canadian Dream is not just another immigration guide filled with generic advice. It is a step-by-step, experience-driven handbook written by someone who has not only lived the struggles of immigration first hand but has also helped thousands achieve their Canadian dreams.

If you are serious about making Canada your home, starting a business, or building a successful career in this thriving economy, then this book is for you.

This book will guide you on the different pathways to migrate, present proven strategies and action plans, and provide clear, honest insights into eligibility criteria and estimated expenses for each approach.

Contents

Chapter - 1

Understanding the Journey of Immigration

Immigrating to a new country is more than just a change of location; it is a complete transformation of one's life. It is a journey filled with hope, ambition, and the pursuit of better opportunities, but it is also accompanied by uncertainties, struggles, and challenges. The decision to leave behind everything familiar; family, friends, traditions, and an established way of life - can be both exhilarating and overwhelming.

For many, Canada represents a land of possibilities, a country that embraces diversity and rewards hard work. But while the promise of a brighter future is strong, the road to establishing a successful life in a foreign country is not always easy. The journey is filled with emotional struggles, financial burdens, and complex bureaucratic processes that require careful navigation. Those who prepare well, adapt quickly, and build strong support networks find themselves thriving in Canada, while those who arrive unprepared often face significant obstacles.

This chapter explores the realities of immigration, the hurdles that newcomers face, and the strategies that can help smoothen the transition. From the emotional toll of leaving home to the financial demands of settling in a new country and the challenges of adapting to an entirely different culture, this section provides a detailed roadmap to help immigrants navigate the early stages of their journey with confidence and resilience.

The Emotional Rollercoaster of Immigration

The moment an individual decides to immigrate, emotions begin to run high. The initial excitement of starting fresh in a new country is often accompanied by fear, anxiety, and uncertainty. Many immigrants grapple with the guilt of leaving behind aging parents, young children, or close-knit communities. The weight of their decision is compounded by the expectations of family members who look up to them as pioneers, hoping they will establish a stable life and, in some cases, provide financial support.

As the departure date draws closer, the reality of leaving home begins to sink in. Saying goodbye to loved ones at the airport is often an emotional moment, one filled with tears, reassurances, and promises of frequent communication. The plane ride to Canada, while a momentous occasion, is also a time of reflection. Questions race through the mind: Will I find a good job? Will I fit into the new culture? Will I be able to build a better life than the one I left behind?

Upon arrival, the initial days can feel overwhelming. Everything feels foreign, the people, the streets, the food, the language, even the way daily life is conducted. Many newcomers experience culture shock, struggling to adjust to unfamiliar customs and social norms. The isolation can be intense, especially for those who arrive without family or friends to support them. Loneliness creeps in, and moments of self-doubt become frequent. There are times when some immigrants wonder if they made the right decision. But amidst the struggles, there are also moments of joy. The first snowfall, the first successful job interview, the first new friend; each small milestone serves as a reminder of why this journey was undertaken in the first place. For those who persist, the emotional rollercoaster gradually stabilizes, and with time, the new country starts to feel like home.

The Financial Challenges of Immigration

For many immigrants, financial stability is one of the biggest concerns when moving to a new country. The cost of immigration can be substantial, and the expenses do not stop once a visa is secured. From visa application fees and airfare to housing, food, and transportation, the financial burden can quickly add up. Many immigrants arrive with limited savings, hoping to secure a job as soon as possible. However, the reality is that finding employment in a foreign country is not always easy, and it may take weeks or even months before a steady income starts coming in.

Solution: Equip yourself with relevant certifications or employability programs that align with current market trends. Focus on networking to increase your chances of job referrals; platforms like LinkedIn can be powerful tools when used strategically. Build a strong profile backed by authentic recommendations.

For students, the financial challenge is even greater. Tuition fees for international students in Canada can be high, and on top of that, there are additional expenses such as rent, food, study materials, and transportation. Many students take up part-time jobs to manage their expenses, but balancing work and studies can be exhausting.

Solution: Consider taking up a part-time job during your studies. Tailor your resume to highlight relevant experience from your home country, even part-time roles count. Enhance your employability by learning in-demand skills like digital marketing, content writing (blogs, articles, social media), and essential life skills that can support remote work opportunities.

Entrepreneurs, on the other hand, have to invest in setting up their businesses, often dealing with unfamiliar regulations and financial systems. For those coming through the Start-Up Visa program, securing funding from incubators and investors is essential, but building a business in a new market requires patience strategy, and an in-depth understanding of the Canadian business landscape.

Solution: Begin by applying for initial grants offered by incubators, angel investors, or venture capital firms. Participate in programs and courses offered by designated organizations to showcase your product or service and gain valuable feedback. Seek mentorship on how to secure funding and build strategic connections within your industry. Canada offers several grants for new startups, including office rental subsidies, digital marketing support, and more.

Financial planning is key to overcoming these challenges. Those who arrive with a well-thought-out financial strategy, one that includes savings, a realistic budget, and an understanding of the cost of living, find it easier to adjust. It is crucial to research affordable housing options, explore government grants or financial aid, and develop a plan for securing employment or business opportunities. The ability to manage money wisely in the first few months can make a significant difference in ensuring long-term stability.

The Challenges of Immigration Paperwork

Understanding Canada's immigration system is a crucial step in the journey, but it can also be one of the most frustrating aspects of moving to a new country. The process is complex, requiring immigrants to navigate through visa applications, work permits, residency paperwork, and legal documentation. Those who fail to prepare in advance often find themselves facing delays, rejections, or difficulties in adjusting to their new environment. The Express Entry system, for example, is one of the fastest ways for skilled workers to gain permanent residency, but not everyone qualifies. The Comprehensive Ranking System (CRS) assigns points based on factors such as age, education, work experience, and language proficiency. Many applicants struggle with low CRS scores, leading them to explore alternative pathways such as the Provincial Nominee Program (PNP), which offers additional opportunities for those with in-demand skills.

Solution: Currently, the CRS score threshold is quite high, often above 500. However, specific sectors such as education, trades, and healthcare have lower draw scores (education: 470+, trades: 430+, healthcare: 410+). Identify which skill category suits you best and explore opportunities to bridge any gaps in your education and work experience to align with immigration priorities.

Students must carefully follow the guidelines for obtaining a study permit, ensuring that all documentation is accurate and up-to-date. Entrepreneurs seeking a Start-Up Visa must meet specific eligibility criteria and secure a Letter of Support from a designated Canadian organization. Those who plan to work in Canada must secure valid work permits and understand their rights as employees under Canadian labor laws. The key to successfully navigating immigration bureaucracy lies in thorough research and proper guidance. Finding a genuine immigration consultant is crucial to your success in the Canadian immigration journey. I've encountered numerous clients from India, the UAE, Canada, and other regions who have fallen victim to scams, misled by consultants promoting Express Entry pathways for which they were never even eligible.

Note: Always verify the credibility of consultants by checking authentic client testimonials and visa approval evidence. For student visas, ask to see actual offer letters and Passport Request Letters (visa approvals). For Start-Up Visa programs, request proof such as letters of support, work permit approvals, business plans, pitch decks, MVPs, progress reports, and compliance reports. Pay close attention to the depth and legitimacy of these documents before proceeding.

Insight: I've come across numerous Start-Up Visa cases where clients received Letters of Support as early as 2019–2020, yet never obtained their Work Permits. Upon further investigation, it became evident that no business bank accounts were opened and no progress or compliance reports had been submitted, clear indicators of an unreliable organization. Consultants must take responsibility for guiding clients through every step with integrity.

Solution: In such cases, judicial review becomes the only recourse. I have personally reviewed and filed multiple judicial review applications, requesting extensions from IRCC to complete due diligence and ensure proper compliance, steps critical to reviving stalled immigration processes.

Adjusting to Canadian Culture and Building a Support Network

Canada's multicultural society makes it one of the most welcoming countries in the world, but that does not mean adjusting to a new culture is easy. Language barriers, social etiquette, workplace expectations, and even the weather can all be significant adjustments. For many immigrants, learning the nuances of Canadian communication styles takes time. Canadians are known for their politeness and indirect way of addressing sensitive topics. In the workplace, collaboration, teamwork, and inclusivity are highly valued, and newcomers must adapt to these expectations to succeed. Finding a sense of belonging is crucial in making Canada feel like home. Many immigrants build strong support networks by connecting with cultural communities, joining professional organizations, and attending networking events. These connections provide not only social support but also valuable guidance on job opportunities, housing, and financial management.

The Journey to Success: Resilience and Adaptability

Immigrating to Canada is not just about reaching a new country; it is about building a new life from the ground up. The process is filled with highs and lows, but those who approach it with a mindset of resilience and adaptability find success. The key is to stay proactive, seek continuous learning opportunities, and embrace the challenges that come with the journey. Those who build strong financial plans, invest in skill development, and establish social connections are the ones who thrive in the long run.

Every successful immigrant once stood at the starting line, facing the same doubts and struggles. The difference lies in preparation, perseverance, and the determination to keep moving forward despite the obstacles. The Canadian dream is within reach for those who are willing to put in the effort. The journey of immigration is not just about moving to a new place; it is about discovering new strengths, overcoming fears, and shaping a future filled with opportunities. And for those who dare to take the leap, Canada is ready to welcome them with open arms.

Overview of the Immigrant Experience in Canada

For many, the decision to immigrate to Canada represents more than just a geographical move; it is the beginning of a new chapter filled with hope, opportunity, and the chance to build a brighter future. Canada has long been celebrated as a land of inclusivity and multiculturalism, a place where people from all walks of life come together to contribute to a thriving and diverse society. However, despite the welcoming environment, the immigrant experience is one of transformation and adaptation, often marked by challenges that require resilience, patience, and a willingness to embrace change.

The journey to Canada does not end upon arrival. In fact, stepping off the plane is just the beginning. Newcomers must navigate a world that is simultaneously welcoming and unfamiliar. The streets are different, the people speak with new accents, and the customs may not always align with what they have known all their lives. There is an adjustment period where everything feels foreign, from the way the weather changes drastically to the unspoken social norms that influence daily interactions. Despite this, Canada offers something invaluable—an opportunity for growth, stability, and success for those who are willing to adapt.

Many immigrants find comfort in the warmth of Canada's diverse communities. The country has long been known for its inclusive immigration policies, and as a result, cities like Toronto, Vancouver, and Montreal are home to large populations of people from countries around the world. Whether it is an Indian grocery store tucked into a suburban neighborhood, a Chinese restaurant serving authentic dumplings, or an Arab bakery filling the air with the scent of freshly baked bread, Canada has become a place where cultures not only coexist but thrive together. For immigrants, this diversity often brings a sense of belonging, a reminder that they are not alone in their journey.

However, the transition to life in Canada is not always seamless. Immigrants quickly realize that while the country offers opportunities, it also demands effort. Securing employment can be a challenge, even for highly skilled professionals with years of experience in their home countries. The Canadian job market often values local experience, and many newcomers struggle to find positions that match their qualifications. It is not uncommon for doctors, engineers, and business executives to take on survival jobs in retail or hospitality while working toward re-establishing their careers. Some face the frustrating reality of credential recognition, where degrees earned abroad may not be immediately accepted in Canada, requiring additional courses or certifications before they can work in their fields.

Financial stability is another concern that weighs heavily on the minds of new immigrants. The cost of living in major cities is high, and without a well-paying job, managing rent, transportation, and daily expenses can be overwhelming. Many immigrants arrive with savings, but without a steady income, those funds deplete quickly. Budgeting becomes crucial in the early months, as every dollar must be carefully allocated to ensure long-term survival. For students, balancing tuition fees with part-time jobs and academic demands is equally challenging, requiring discipline and careful planning. Entrepreneurs, too, face financial hurdles as they work to understand the Canadian business landscape, secure funding, and establish their ventures in a competitive market. Despite these difficulties, immigrants often find relief in the support systems available to them. Canada offers a range of settlement programs designed to help newcomers integrate into society. Nonprofit organizations provide language training, job search assistance, and community services to ease the transition. Many immigrants turn to these resources to develop their skills, build professional networks, and gain an understanding of how Canadian workplaces function. These services become lifelines, bridging the gap between struggle and success.

Adapting to the social and cultural norms of Canada is another important aspect of the immigrant experience. The country values politeness, inclusivity, and respect for individual rights, which can sometimes be an adjustment for those coming from societies with different customs and traditions. Small things, such as making eye contact during conversations, greeting strangers with a smile, or understanding the importance of personal space, can feel unfamiliar at first. Workplace culture, too, presents a learning curve, with expectations of teamwork, open communication, and work-life balance differing from those in many other countries. Over time, immigrants begin to recognize and appreciate these aspects of Canadian life, gradually incorporating them into their own daily interactions.

Language barriers can add another layer of difficulty to integration. While many immigrants arrive in Canada with English or French proficiency, others struggle to communicate effectively, making it harder to find jobs, access services, and build relationships. For those who do not speak the official languages fluently, the first few months can feel isolating. Attending language classes, practicing daily conversations, and engaging with local communities become essential steps in overcoming this obstacle. As language skills improve, confidence grows, opening up new opportunities for career advancement and social engagement.

Education is one of the strongest pillars supporting immigrant success in Canada. The country is home to some of the world's top-ranked universities and colleges, attracting thousands of international students each year. For young immigrants, higher education is often seen as a pathway to permanent residency and long-term stability. The experience of studying in Canada is an eye-opening one, exposing students to new perspectives, critical thinking, and global networks that will shape their future careers. For families with children, Canada's free public education system provides access to quality learning opportunities, ensuring that the next generation has the tools to succeed in a competitive world.

For individuals migrating to Canada on a Permanent Residency or Work Permit, it's important to understand the wide range of educational opportunities available. Those residing in Canada under these statuses may be eligible for government grants to help cover educational expenses. Additionally, various loan options are also available to support further studies, empowering newcomers to enhance their skills and career prospects.

One of the most reassuring aspects of life in Canada for immigrants is the access to free healthcare. Unlike in many countries where medical expenses can be a significant burden, Canada's publicly funded healthcare system ensures that residents receive necessary medical services without the fear of overwhelming bills. While there may be wait times for certain procedures, the fact that healthcare is accessible and available provides a sense of security to those building their new lives. As immigrants settle into their new environment, they begin to see the rewards of their hard work and perseverance. The struggles of the early days give way to small victories landing a first job, finding a comfortable place to live, making new friends, and gaining confidence in navigating the system. These achievements build a sense of belonging, reinforcing the idea that Canada is not just a temporary stop but a true home.

The success of immigrants in Canada is often determined by their mindset. Those who approach the journey with resilience, adaptability, and a willingness to learn are the ones who thrive. They seek opportunities where others see obstacles, they network, upskill, and immerse themselves in the local culture. They do not give up when faced with difficulties but instead find ways to overcome them. It is this spirit of determination that allows immigrants to carve out a place for themselves in Canadian society, contributing not only to their own personal success but also to the growth and prosperity of the country as a whole. The immigrant experience in Canada is a journey of transformation. It is a process of letting go of the familiar, stepping into the unknown, and gradually shaping a future filled with possibilities. The road may be challenging, but for those who stay the course, Canada offers a wealth of opportunities that make every struggle worth it. With the right preparation, determination, and an open mindset, immigrants can turn their dreams into reality, building lives that are not just successful but deeply fulfilling.

Backdoor Entry to the USA: The Legal Pathways from Canada

For many ambitious students, skilled professionals, and entrepreneurs, the ultimate goal is not just to immigrate to Canada but to use it as a stepping stone to enter the United States. The United States remains one of the most sought-after destinations for career growth, business expansion, and world-class education. While securing a direct U.S. visa can be challenging due to strict immigration policies and high competition, Canada offers a unique advantage: several structured and legal pathways that can lead to U.S. residency or work opportunities. The term "backdoor entry" often implies an informal or unauthorized route, but in the context of Canadian immigration, it refers to legitimate and well-established pathways that allow immigrants and business owners in Canada to transition into the U.S. under specific visa categories. The close economic and diplomatic relationship between the two nations has led to agreements that make this possible, especially for those who have established themselves in Canada through work permits, permanent residency, or business ventures.

The U.S.-Canada Relationship: A Unique Advantage for Immigrants

The geographical proximity and historical ties between Canada and the U.S. have created a framework for simplified immigration processes between the two countries. Unlike applicants from other nations who must navigate the complex U.S. visa system from scratch, individuals residing in Canada, especially those with Canadian permanent residency or work experience, have an advantage when applying for U.S. visas. For decades, Canada has served as a strategic gateway for immigrants looking to move to the United States. Many multinational companies have offices in both countries, making employee transfers smoother. Trade agreements such as the United States-Mexico-Canada Agreement (USMCA), formerly NAFTA, facilitate business and professional exchanges, creating specific visa categories for Canadian-based professionals and entrepreneurs.

The key to leveraging Canada as a stepping stone to the U.S. lies in understanding the immigration options available and planning a career or business strategy accordingly.

The U.S. Visa Waiver Program for Canadians

Canada and the United States share one of the closest international relationships in the world, built on decades of economic, social, and political cooperation. This unique partnership has led to a series of agreements that allow for easier movement between the two nations, particularly for Canadian citizens. The U.S. Visa Waiver Program (VWP) is one such initiative that enables certain travelers to visit the United States for tourism or business without needing to apply for a traditional visa. While the VWP is commonly used by citizens of several countries, Canadians benefit from even more streamlined travel privileges. However, permanent residents of Canada who are not Canadian citizens do not qualify for the same ease of entry and must follow a separate process to obtain a visa.

For many individuals, moving to Canada is the first step in a larger plan to gain access to the United States. Whether they are students aiming for educational opportunities, entrepreneurs looking for business expansion, or skilled professionals seeking employment, the strategic advantage of being in Canada opens doors that may otherwise remain closed. Understanding the U.S. Visa Waiver Program and its limitations is critical for those who see Canada as a pathway to broader opportunities in North America.

How the U.S. Visa Waiver Program Works for Canadian

Canadian citizens enjoy one of the most straightforward travel processes to the United States. Unlike citizens of other countries who require approval under the Electronic System for Travel Authorization (ESTA) to participate in the Visa Waiver Program, Canadian passport holders do not need pre-authorization for short visits to the U.S. They can enter the country freely for business or leisure, staying for up to 90 days at a time without the need for a visa. This makes travel for networking, business meetings, tourism, and short-term educational programs incredibly convenient.

For professionals and business owners, this flexibility is a major advantage. Canadian entrepreneurs can explore investment opportunities, attend trade fairs, and connect with potential clients and partners without having to navigate the complexities of a U.S. visa application. Likewise, skilled workers who are looking to assess career opportunities in the United States can attend job interviews and industry conferences with ease. However, while the program allows for short-term visits, it does not provide authorization for employment, study, or long-term stays. Canadians who wish to work or study in the U.S. must apply for the appropriate visa category.

Pathways to Canada: Unlocking Opportunities Through Education, Work, and Investment

Canada has earned its reputation as one of the most immigrant-friendly nations in the world, offering numerous pathways for individuals looking to build a future in the country. Whether you are a student seeking world-class education, a skilled worker eager to explore career prospects, an entrepreneur hoping to launch a business, or an investor searching for lucrative opportunities, Canada provides structured and legal immigration programs tailored to meet these aspirations. Each route comes with its own benefits, requirements, and long-term opportunities, making it essential for aspiring immigrants to choose the pathway that best aligns with their goals.

For students, the education route offers a strong foundation for long-term success, allowing them to gain valuable qualifications and seamlessly transition into the workforce. Skilled professionals can take advantage of the Express Entry system, one of the fastest and most efficient immigration programs in the world. Those looking for immediate employment can explore LMIA-based jobs, while entrepreneurs with innovative business ideas can benefit from the Start-Up Visa. Investors with significant capital can choose the Investment Visa, which grants permanent residency based on economic contributions to the country.

Navigating these immigration options requires careful planning, strategic decision-making, and a clear understanding of the process. Each pathway offers a unique experience, and choosing the right one can be the key to achieving success and stability in Canada.

Education route to migrate to Canada

For many international students, studying in Canada is more than just an academic experience; it is a stepping stone to building a long-term career and securing permanent residency. Canadian universities and colleges are recognized worldwide for their high standards of education, state-of-the-art research facilities, and strong industry connections. As a result, Canada has become a top destination for students from around the globe, particularly from India, China, the Philippines, and Nigeria. The education route provides several advantages for aspiring immigrants. Unlike other immigration pathways that require a pre-existing job offer or investment capital, studying in Canada allows students to establish themselves in the country, gain Canadian work experience, and integrate into society before applying for permanent residency. International students are also eligible for work permits during and after their studies, making it easier for them to build a professional network and gain financial stability.

A significant benefit of studying in Canada is the Post-Graduation Work Permit (PGWP), which allows graduates to work in Canada for up to three years after completing their program. This work experience is crucial when applying for permanent residency through programs like the Canadian Experience Class (CEC) under the Express Entry system. Many students take advantage of this opportunity to gain valuable industry experience, making them highly competitive candidates for PR.

Moreover, Canada has a relatively straightforward pathway for students to transition from temporary residence to permanent residency. Several provinces have immigration programs specifically designed for international graduates, including the Ontario Immigrant Nominee Program (OINP), the British Columbia Provincial Nominee Program (BCPNP), and the Atlantic Immigration Program (AIP). These programs prioritize candidates who have studied in Canada, making it easier for them to secure PR without needing extensive work experience.

Express Entry

Express Entry is one of the most efficient and competitive immigration programs in the world, offering skilled professionals the opportunity to become permanent residents in Canada. It is a points-based system that evaluates candidates based on factors such as age, education, work experience, and language proficiency. Those who score high on the Comprehensive Ranking System (CRS) receive an Invitation to Apply (ITA) for permanent residency, making the process faster and more transparent than many other immigration programs.

The Express Entry system is divided into three main categories: the Federal Skilled Worker Program (FSWP), the Federal Skilled Trades Program (FSTP), and the Canadian Experience Class (CEC). Each category caters to different types of professionals, ensuring that skilled workers in various industries can find a pathway that suits their qualifications. One of the biggest advantages of Express Entry is that candidates do not necessarily need a job offer to apply. However, those who have arranged employment in Canada receive additional CRS points, significantly increasing their chances of receiving an ITA. Additionally, applicants with strong academic backgrounds, high language proficiency scores, and prior work experience in Canada have a competitive edge in the selection process.

The processing time for Express Entry applications is relatively quick, often taking as little as six months for successful candidates to receive permanent residency. This makes it an attractive option for skilled workers who wish to settle in Canada with minimal delays. Many immigrants who enter Canada through Express Entry find themselves on a fast track to career success, as permanent residency grants them access to the same rights and benefits as Canadian citizens, including healthcare, social security, and the ability to sponsor family members.

My Insights: While Express Entry remains one of the fastest immigration pathways to Canada, it's essential to understand the nuances of the program. It may not be ideal for individuals over the age of 30, as CRS points decline significantly with age. Typically, to achieve a competitive score of 470+, candidates need to meet **three key criteria:**

- Master's Degree
- IELTS Score 8777
- Age Less than 30 years. However, with current draw scores hovering around 510+, meeting these requirements alone may not be sufficient. So how do you bridge the gap? The answer lies in exploring alternative options such as LMIA-supported job offers, the Start-Up Visa, trade-specific programs, education-focused draws, healthcare pathways, or Provincial Nominee Programs (PNPs).

LMIA Jobs

For those who may not qualify for Express Entry due to lower CRS scores, obtaining a job offer from a Canadian employer can be a game-changer. The Labour Market Impact Assessment (LMIA) process allows employers to hire foreign workers when no qualified Canadian citizens or permanent residents are available to fill a specific position. A positive LMIA strengthens an applicant's Express Entry profile by adding additional CRS points, significantly improving their chances of receiving an ITA for permanent residency.

LMIA-based jobs are particularly beneficial for professionals in high-demand industries such as healthcare, engineering, IT, and skilled trades. Employers seeking to hire foreign workers must demonstrate that the job cannot be filled by a Canadian citizen or permanent resident and that hiring an international worker will have a positive impact on the labor market. Once an LMIA is approved, the foreign worker can apply for a work permit and begin working in Canada, gaining valuable experience that enhances their long-term immigration prospects. Many LMIA job holders eventually transition to permanent residency through Express Entry or Provincial Nominee Programs (PNPs). Some provinces even have LMIA-exempt pathways for foreign workers, allowing them to apply for PR directly without the need for additional work experience. For individuals who are determined to work in Canada and eventually obtain PR, securing an LMIA job is an excellent strategy.

Insight: Be cautious when pursuing LMIA-based opportunities. Always verify the authenticity of the employer and the validity of the job offer. Unfortunately, immigration scams involving fraudulent job offers are increasingly common, and due diligence is essential to avoid falling victim.

Start-Up Visa

Entrepreneurs with an innovative business ideas can take advantage of Canada's Start-Up Visa program, which offers permanent residency to those who can secure the backing of a designated venture capitalist, angel investor group, or business incubator. This program is designed to attract entrepreneurs who have the potential to create jobs, contribute to economic growth, and compete on a global scale. Unlike traditional business immigration programs that require large investment capital, the Start-Up Visa focuses on innovation and scalability. The key requirement is securing a letter of support from a designated organization that is willing to invest in or mentor the business. Entrepreneurs who meet this criterion can apply for PR even before their business becomes fully operational.

The Start-Up Visa program is particularly attractive to tech entrepreneurs, as Canada has a thriving startup ecosystem with strong government support, funding opportunities, and a growing market for innovation. Many successful businesses in AI, fintech, and e-commerce have emerged from the Start-Up Visa program, demonstrating its potential for long-term success.

Note: The Start-Up Visa is currently the only Canadian immigration program that does not rely on the CRS or a points-based system. It offers a distinct pathway to permanent residency and serves as a bridge for start-ups and bootstrapped ventures looking to expand in Canada. Beyond the immigration benefits, the program provides access to funding through venture capitalists, angel investors, and business incubators. Additionally, numerous support platforms are available, ranging from free office space and rental subsidies to digital marketing assistance and campaign reimbursements, making it a comprehensive launchpad for innovative entrepreneurs.

Investment Visa

For high-net-worth individuals looking to migrate to Canada, the Investment Visa provides an opportunity to obtain permanent residency by making a significant economic contribution to the country. The Quebec Immigrant Investor Program (QIIP) is one of the most well-known options, requiring applicants to invest a substantial amount in government-approved projects while meeting specific net worth criteria.

Other investment programs are available in provinces such as British Columbia, Alberta, and Ontario. Investors who choose to invest in rural or smaller communities often benefit from special incentives, including rebates and fast-track immigration options. For instance, rural communities in Ontario,, such as Sudbury, offer unique opportunities for investment-led immigration. Similarly, Manitoba is increasingly attracting investors due to its practical and cost-effective investment plans.

Investment-based immigration is an excellent choice for business owners, executives, and investors who want to gain Canadian residency without going through traditional work or study routes. The program offers a straightforward path to PR, with minimal residency obligations, making it ideal for those who want to maintain global business operations while securing a future in Canada.

Canada's diverse immigration pathways offer something for everyone, from students and professionals to entrepreneurs and investors. Understanding the benefits and requirements of each program is crucial for making informed decisions and maximizing the chances of success. Whether you are looking to study, work, start a business, or invest, Canada provides the tools and opportunities to help you achieve your immigration goals.

Chapter - 2
Canada vs. The World: The Ultimate Choice for Immigrants

Canada has earned its place as one of the most desirable destinations for immigrants worldwide. Its reputation as a country that welcomes diversity, values hard work, and offers economic stability makes it a top choice for students, professionals, and entrepreneurs seeking a better life. While other nations, such as the United States, the United Kingdom, Australia, and Germany, also offer immigration opportunities, Canada stands out for its well-structured immigration system, multicultural society, and strong government support for newcomers.

The decision to immigrate is not just about securing a visa, it is about choosing a country where long-term success and personal fulfillment are possible. For many, the ultimate question becomes: why Canada over other countries? The answer lies not only in the economic opportunities available but also in the social and cultural environment that makes Canada a true land of opportunity. Immigrants are not merely tolerated in Canada; they are embraced, valued, and integrated into the fabric of society. This welcoming environment, combined with a transparent immigration process, makes Canada a destination of choice for millions around the world. Canada's appeal is not limited to any single group. Students are drawn to its world-class universities and post-graduation work opportunities. Skilled professionals are attracted to the high-paying job market and the promise of permanent residency. Entrepreneurs see Canada as a fertile ground for business growth, supported by government-backed funding, tax incentives, and access to global markets. Even investors find Canada to be a stable and secure destination for wealth preservation and growth. *The Canadian Dream* is not a vague promise; it is a tangible reality backed by a strong economy, a fair legal system, and a government that actively supports immigrants.

Why Students Prefer Canada

Canada has become one of the most popular destinations for international students, with over 600,000 students from around the world enrolled in Canadian universities and colleges. Its reputation for academic excellence, combined with affordable tuition rates and generous post-graduation work opportunities, makes it an attractive option for students seeking long-term success. Unlike countries like the United States and the United Kingdom, where student visas are often restrictive and provide limited work options, Canada allows international students to work part-time while studying and grants them the ability to stay and work after graduation through the Post-Graduation Work Permit (PGWP) program. This program allows graduates to gain Canadian work experience, which strengthens their eligibility for permanent residency under the Canadian Experience Class (CEC) of the Express Entry system.

Currently, one of the most promising immigration pathways for international students is the Skilled Trades route, which offers strong support for obtaining permanent residency. This pathway significantly enhances the chances of immigration for students engaged in skilled trades such as

- Carpenter
- Painter
- Truck Driver
- Chef
- Cook…and many others. For a comprehensive list of eligible occupations, refer to the official IRCC website.

Canadian universities consistently rank among the best in the world, offering a wide range of programs in fields such as engineering, business, healthcare, and information technology. Institutions such as the University of Toronto, McGill University, and the University of British Columbia have produced global leaders in business, science, and politics.

The quality of education in Canada is matched by the diversity of its student population, creating an environment where students from different cultural backgrounds can learn from one another and build global networks.

Affordability is another key factor driving students to Canada. While the cost of education in Canada is not the lowest in the world, it is significantly more affordable than tuition fees in the United States and the United Kingdom. Additionally, Canada offers numerous scholarships and financial aid programs to support international students, helping them manage their expenses and focus on their studies. The path from student to permanent resident is one of the most structured and transparent in the world. After completing their studies, international students who secure full-time jobs in Canada can apply for permanent residency through Express Entry or Provincial Nominee Programs (PNPs). The combination of academic excellence, work opportunities, and a clear path to residency makes Canada the ultimate destination for students seeking both education and long-term career success.

Why Professionals Prefer Canada

Canada's labor market is one of the strongest in the world, with consistent demand for skilled workers across industries such as healthcare, technology, finance, and engineering. Unlike countries where work visas are tied to specific employers or industries, Canada's immigration system gives skilled professionals the flexibility to change jobs, advance their careers, and even start their own businesses after securing permanent residency. The Express Entry system is the backbone of Canada's skilled worker immigration program. It evaluates candidates based on factors such as age, education, work experience, and language proficiency, assigning them a Comprehensive Ranking System (CRS) score. Those with the highest scores receive Invitations to Apply (ITA) for permanent residency, with the entire process often taking less than six months.

Canada's immigration system values work experience gained within the country, making it easier for professionals who have already worked in Canada to transition to permanent residency. Many professionals begin their journey by obtaining a work permit through the Labour Market

Impact Assessment (LMIA) process, which allows Canadian employers to hire foreign workers when no qualified local candidates are available. Once they have accumulated sufficient work experience, these professionals become highly competitive candidates for permanent residency through Express Entry.

The Canadian job market is particularly strong for professionals in the technology sector. Cities like Toronto, Vancouver, and Montreal have become major hubs for artificial intelligence, software development, and cybersecurity. The Global Talent Stream program allows Canadian employers to fast-track the hiring of skilled tech workers, offering work permits in as little as two weeks. This streamlined process gives tech professionals a significant advantage in securing employment and residency in Canada. Healthcare is another sector where demand for skilled workers remains consistently high. Nurses, doctors, medical technicians, and healthcare administrators are in short supply across Canada, leading to numerous job openings and fast-tracked immigration options. The healthcare sector also benefits from government funding and support, ensuring that professionals working in this field have access to resources and career growth opportunities.

The ability to bring family members to Canada is another significant advantage for skilled professionals. Unlike other countries where work visas are often restricted to the primary applicant, Canada allows work permit holders to sponsor their spouses and dependent children. This family-friendly approach enhances the overall immigration experience and makes it easier for professionals to build a stable and fulfilling life in Canada.

Why Businessmen Prefer Canada as Their Destination for Business Growth: Top Reasons

Canada has established itself as one of the most attractive destinations for entrepreneurs and business professionals worldwide. Its stable political environment, robust economy, and transparent business regulations make it an ideal location for starting, expanding, and growing a business. For decades, Canada has been recognized not only for its natural beauty and high quality of life but also for its thriving business ecosystem, which offers strategic advantages to those who seek to build global businesses.

Businessmen from all over the world are drawn to Canada because of the numerous benefits it provides, including global recognition, easier entry into the United States, faster settlement opportunities, and a multicultural society that embraces diversity. The Canadian government actively supports entrepreneurship by offering funding options through government grants, banks, angel investors, and venture capitalists. These factors create a highly competitive and supportive business environment that allows immigrant entrepreneurs to thrive.

Unlike other countries where starting a business as a foreign national can be an uphill battle due to restrictive regulations, Canada welcomes entrepreneurs with open arms. The Start-Up Visa program, for example, is one of the most accessible and entrepreneur-friendly immigration programs in the world. This program reflects Canada's commitment to attracting and retaining business talent by providing permanent residency to those who have innovative business ideas and the potential to create jobs for Canadians.

For business-minded individuals, Canada offers not only a pathway to permanent residency but also a strategic advantage in accessing the North American market. Its close relationship with the United States and participation in trade agreements such as the United States-Mexico-Canada Agreement (USMCA) provide business owners with unparalleled access to one of the largest consumer markets in the world. This combination of market access, government support, and a welcoming business environment positions Canada as a top destination for entrepreneurs and business professionals.

Global Recognition

One of the key reasons businessmen prefer Canada is the global recognition that comes with operating a business in the country. Canada is consistently ranked among the top countries for business environment, economic stability, and ease of doing business. Its strong international reputation extends to its financial sector, regulatory system, and intellectual property protections, which make it easier for Canadian businesses to secure international partnerships and investments. When a business is established in Canada, it gains instant credibility on the global stage. International investors and business partners are more likely to engage with Canadian businesses because of the country's strong legal framework and transparent business practices. The Canadian government has created an environment where businesses can operate with confidence, knowing that their intellectual property, contracts, and business dealings are protected by law.

Canadian businesses benefit from a robust legal system that enforces contracts and protects property rights. Unlike in some developing countries where legal disputes can take years to resolve, Canada offers a fair and efficient judicial system that ensures business owners can focus on growing their enterprises without worrying about legal complications. This stability and protection give Canadian businesses a competitive edge when engaging in international trade and securing foreign investments. Canada's membership in global trade organizations such as the World Trade Organization (WTO) and its participation in major trade agreements such as the Comprehensive and Progressive Agreement for Trans-Pacific Partnership (CPTPP) further enhance its global standing. These trade agreements open up new markets for Canadian businesses, allowing them to expand beyond North America and establish a presence in Asia, Europe, and other key regions.

For immigrant entrepreneurs, the global recognition associated with running a business in Canada translates into greater opportunities for growth and expansion. A Canadian business address or headquarters signals to potential partners and clients that the business operates in a stable, transparent, and competitive market. This credibility makes it easier to attract funding, establish strategic partnerships, and secure contracts with international clients.

Entry to USA

One of the most significant strategic advantages of starting a business in Canada is the access it provides to the U.S. market. Canada and the United States share the longest undefended border in the world and maintain one of the closest economic relationships globally. The United

States-Mexico-Canada Agreement (USMCA) allows Canadian businesses to trade with minimal tariffs and restrictions, giving Canadian-based companies a competitive advantage when expanding into the U.S.

For immigrant entrepreneurs, this means that establishing a business in Canada can serve as a direct pathway to the U.S. market. Unlike businesses from other countries that face complex regulations and trade barriers when entering the U.S., Canadian businesses benefit from simplified customs processes and preferential trade treatment. Products and services developed in Canada can be easily exported to the U.S., opening up access to a consumer market of over 330 million people.

The TN visa program, which falls under the USMCA, allows Canadian business professionals and skilled workers to work in the U.S. without going through the complex H-1B visa lottery process. Entrepreneurs who establish successful businesses in Canada can leverage the TN visa to expand their operations into the U.S. and transfer key employees between their Canadian and American branches. This streamlined mobility between Canada and the U.S. gives Canadian businesses a significant operational advantage.

The L-1 visa program also benefits Canadian business owners looking to enter the U.S. market. Business owners who establish a company in Canada and have been operating it for at least one year can transfer executives and key personnel to a U.S. branch under the L-1 visa. This program allows Canadian entrepreneurs to scale their businesses across North America without needing to go through the lengthy U.S. immigration process. The ability to access the U.S. market through Canada is a game-changer for entrepreneurs. It allows them to test their business models in Canada's diverse and supportive environment before expanding into the highly competitive U.S. market. The strategic advantage of using Canada as a launchpad for North American expansion makes it one of the most attractive destinations for business growth.

Another emerging and increasingly popular option is the E2 Visa, which allows Canadian citizens to establish a business in the United States and obtain a Green Card within a relatively short period, typically 1 to 2 years. This program is especially attractive because it requires a comparatively modest investment of around USD 100,000, unlike the EB-5 visa, which demands a minimum of USD 1 million. Qualifying investments can include small businesses such as restaurants, coffee shops, or even specialty retail stores like candy shops.

Faster Settlement

Canada's immigration system is designed to help business owners and skilled professionals settle quickly and start contributing to the economy without unnecessary delays. The Start-Up Visa program, in particular, offers one of the fastest routes to permanent residency for entrepreneurs. Once a business owner secures a Letter of Support from a designated organization (such as an incubator, venture capital fund, or angel investor), they can apply for permanent residency and begin operating their business in Canada.

Unlike other countries where business immigration programs require long processing times and complex bureaucratic processes, Canada's Start-Up Visa program is efficient and streamlined. Business owners who meet the eligibility criteria can expect to receive permanent residency within 12 to 18 months, allowing them to focus on growing their business rather than navigating immigration hurdles.

Note: Kindly refer the IRCC website for any timeline changes to the program.

The Canadian Experience Class (CEC) under the Express Entry system also allows skilled professionals to settle quickly and transition to permanent residency after gaining work experience in Canada. Business owners who employ skilled workers in Canada can benefit from this program by retaining their talent and helping their employees secure permanent residency status. Canada's fast-track settlement process extends beyond immigration. Newcomers receive support through government-funded settlement services, which help them find housing, access healthcare, and integrate into the local community. This comprehensive support system ensures that business owners can focus on growing their enterprises while their families adjust to life in Canada.

Multiculturalism

Canada's commitment to multiculturalism is one of its most defining characteristics. Unlike other countries where immigrants may face discrimination or social barriers, Canada actively promotes diversity and inclusion. This welcoming environment makes it easier for immigrant business owners to integrate into society, establish networks, and build successful businesses.

The multicultural nature of Canada also creates a unique consumer market where businesses can cater to diverse communities. Entrepreneurs who understand the cultural preferences and needs of different ethnic groups can carve out profitable market niches and build loyal customer bases. Restaurants, retail stores, and service-based businesses that reflect the cultural diversity of Canada often perform exceptionally well.

Government policies supporting multiculturalism extend to business regulations and hiring practices. Canadian businesses are encouraged to adopt inclusive hiring practices and create diverse work environments. Business owners who prioritize diversity and inclusion are often eligible for government grants and funding, further strengthening their business operations.

Growing Business Opportunities

Canada's business landscape is characterized by diversity and growth. Unlike many economies that are dependent on a single industry, Canada has a balanced and diversified economic structure that allows businesses across multiple sectors to succeed. From technology and healthcare to natural resources and financial services, Canada's economic ecosystem provides opportunities for entrepreneurs with a wide range of expertise and business models.

One of the primary reasons why businessmen prefer Canada is the country's strategic position in the global economy. Canada's participation in major trade agreements including the United States-Mexico-Canada Agreement (USMCA) and the Comprehensive and Progressive Agreement for Trans-Pacific Partnership (CPTPP), allows Canadian businesses to access markets across North America and the

Asia-Pacific region with reduced trade barriers. This gives Canadian businesses a competitive advantage, allowing them to expand internationally and reach millions of consumers without facing high tariffs or regulatory obstacles.

The technology sector in Canada has become one of the fastest-growing industries in the country. Cities like Toronto, Vancouver, and Montreal have emerged as global hubs for artificial intelligence, software development, and financial technology (fintech). The Canadian government has recognized the potential of the tech sector and has introduced targeted immigration programs, such as the Global Talent Stream, to attract highly skilled tech professionals from around the world. This influx of talent has created a thriving ecosystem for technology-based startups, making it easier for new businesses to scale quickly.

Healthcare and life sciences are other high-growth industries in Canada. The country's aging population has created a rising demand for healthcare services, medical technology, and pharmaceutical products. Entrepreneurs who enter the healthcare sector in Canada find themselves in a market with strong demand and significant government support. The Canadian government invests heavily in healthcare infrastructure, creating opportunities for businesses that provide innovative solutions to meet the growing needs of the healthcare system.

The natural resources sector, including oil, gas, and mining, remains a cornerstone of the Canadian economy. Canada's vast reserves of natural resources and its commitment to sustainable development create opportunities for businesses involved in energy production, environmental technology, and resource management. Entrepreneurs who introduce innovative solutions in renewable energy and environmental conservation find themselves well-positioned for success in Canada's resource-based economy. The food and beverage industry has also experienced significant growth in Canada. The country's multicultural population creates demand for a diverse range of food products and dining experiences. Entrepreneurs in the food industry benefit from Canada's strong agricultural base, which ensures a steady supply of high-quality ingredients. Additionally, the rise of e-commerce and food delivery services has created new business models for food entrepreneurs, allowing them to reach customers through online platforms and mobile apps.

Retail and e-commerce represent another area of growing business opportunities in Canada. The shift toward online shopping and digital marketing has opened new avenues for business owners to reach customers and increase sales. Canadian consumers have embraced online shopping, creating opportunities for businesses involved in logistics, digital marketing, and product development. The Canadian government's support for e-commerce businesses, including grants and training programs, further enhances the potential for success in this sector.

Entrepreneurs in Canada also benefit from the country's thriving real estate market. While housing prices in major cities like Toronto and Vancouver have increased in recent years, the demand for residential and commercial properties remains strong. Business owners who invest in real estate development, property management, and construction-related services find themselves in a market with consistent demand and opportunities for high returns on investment. The diversity and strength of Canada's economy ensure that business owners from all industries can find opportunities for growth and success. The government's commitment to creating a business-friendly environment, combined with strong market demand and access to international trade, positions Canada as one of the most attractive destinations for business growth in the world.

Funding for Businesses from the Government and Banks

One of the most significant advantages of starting a business in Canada is the availability of funding from government programs and financial institutions. The Canadian government recognizes the importance of small and medium-sized enterprises (SMEs) in driving economic growth and has introduced several initiatives to support business development. Unlike in many other countries where securing funding can be a major hurdle for immigrant entrepreneurs, Canada offers a structured and accessible system for obtaining capital.

The Canada Small Business Financing Program (CSBFP) is one of the most widely used government programs for business funding. Through this program, small businesses can access loans of up to $1 million for the purpose of purchasing equipment, expanding operations, or improving cash flow. The government guarantees up to 85% of the loan amount, reducing the risk for financial institutions and making it easier for business owners to secure financing. The Industrial Research Assistance Program (IRAP) provides funding for businesses involved in research and development (R&D). Entrepreneurs who introduce innovative products, services, or technologies can apply for IRAP funding to cover the costs of product development, market research, and commercialization. The program reflects Canada's commitment to fostering innovation and technological advancement.

Canadian banks and credit unions also play a major role in supporting business growth. Major financial institutions such as RBC, TD Bank, and Scotiabank offer business loans, lines of credit, and commercial mortgages tailored to the needs of entrepreneurs. Business owners with a strong business plan and a clear growth strategy have access to competitive interest rates and flexible repayment terms. Government-backed grants and subsidies further strengthen Canada's funding ecosystem. Programs like the Strategic Innovation Fund (SIF) and the Export Development Canada (EDC) fund provide capital to businesses involved in key industries such as technology, renewable energy, and international trade. The government's willingness to invest in business development reflects its recognition of the critical role that entrepreneurs play in driving economic growth and job creation.

Angel Investors, Venture Capitalists, and Business Incubators

In addition to government support and bank loans, Canadian entrepreneurs benefit from a strong network of private investors and business incubators. Angel investors and venture capitalists are highly active in Canada, particularly in the technology sector. Entrepreneurs who demonstrate high growth potential and scalability often attract investment from private funding sources, which provides not only capital but also strategic guidance and industry expertise. Business incubators and accelerators are another valuable resource for entrepreneurs in Canada. These organizations provide early-stage businesses with office space, funding, mentorship, and networking opportunities. Leading incubators such as MaRS Discovery District in Toronto and the Creative Destruction Lab in Vancouver have helped launch some of Canada's most successful startups.

The combination of government support, private investment, and strategic business guidance creates an environment where entrepreneurs can test, refine, and scale their business models quickly. For immigrant business owners, access to this ecosystem is a game-changer. It allows them to compete in the Canadian market while building the foundation for long-term success. Canada's business ecosystem reflects a unique balance of government backing, private investment, and strategic support. Entrepreneurs and business professionals who choose to start their journey in Canada find themselves in a market that values innovation, rewards hard work, and provides the resources needed to succeed. This combination of factors makes Canada one of the most attractive destinations for business growth and long-term prosperity.

Author's Insight

The Start-Up Visa is one of the most effective platforms for securing funding from venture capitalists, angel investors, and business incubators. Success under this program requires a truly innovative business plan, often involving cutting-edge technologies like Artificial Intelligence, Machine Learning, or other first-of-their-kind solutions.

Having worked on over 72 Start-Up Visa projects, I've witnessed funding being granted even at the conceptual stage. I've personally assisted numerous start-ups in securing various forms of support, including free office space, rental reimbursements, digital marketing assistance, Meta Ads funding, and investments of up to CAD 2 million.

Chapter - 3

Navigating Safely: Avoiding Immigration Scams in Canada

The journey to Canadian residency or citizenship is not without its challenges. Among the biggest threats that immigrants face are fraudulent agents and immigration scams. Every year, thousands of hopeful applicants fall victim to unscrupulous individuals and agencies who exploit the complexity of Canada's immigration system for personal gain. These scams often promise guaranteed visas, fast-tracked permanent residency, or insider access to immigration officials, claims that are not only false but can also have severe legal and financial consequences.

The rise in immigration scams is partly due to the growing demand for Canadian immigration. Canada's welcoming immigration policies, strong labor market, and high standard of living have made it one of the most sought-after destinations for migrants worldwide. However, the very complexity of Canada's immigration system; combined with the high volume of applicants; has created an opportunity for fraudsters to exploit vulnerable individuals. Scammers target students seeking study permits, skilled workers applying through Express Entry, entrepreneurs exploring the Start-Up Visa program, and families hoping to sponsor relatives.

The emotional and financial toll of falling victim to an immigration scam can be devastating. Applicants who are misled into paying large sums of money for fake job offers or fraudulent immigration services often find themselves not only losing money but also jeopardizing their chances of legally immigrating to Canada. In some cases, applicants who unknowingly submit false information due to bad advice may face bans from entering Canada altogether.

We will explore the most common types of immigration scams in Canada, how to recognize them, and the steps immigrants can take to protect themselves. Knowledge and awareness are the most powerful tools in avoiding scams and ensuring a successful immigration journey. By understanding the structure of Canada's immigration system and relying on legitimate resources, applicants can safeguard themselves from fraudulent schemes and pursue their Canadian dream with confidence.

Understanding the Reality of Express Entry and Immigration Challenges

Express Entry is one of Canada's most popular and competitive immigration ways, designed to attract skilled workers who can contribute to the country's economy. However, the program is not as straightforward as some agents and consultants may lead applicants to believe. Express Entry operates on a points-based system called the Comprehensive Ranking System (CRS), which evaluates applicants based on factors such as age, education, work experience, language proficiency, and adaptability.

To receive an Invitation to Apply (ITA) for permanent residency through Express Entry, applicants must have a high CRS score. In recent years, the minimum cutoff for receiving an ITA has been increasingly competitive, often exceeding 520 points. This has made it more difficult for applicants with average scores to qualify. Scammers take advantage of this reality by offering false promises of guaranteed success. Some fraudulent agents claim to have "connections" within the immigration system or insider access that can influence the outcome of an application. In reality, Canada's immigration process is strictly regulated, and decisions are based solely on the merit of the application as assessed through the CRS. No consultant or agent can manipulate the outcome of an Express Entry application.

Applicants who struggle to meet the CRS cutoff may be tempted to explore alternative options presented by agents, such as fake job offers or fabricated credentials. These approaches are not only illegal but also highly risky. If discovered, they can result in application rejection, entry bans, and even legal consequences.

The Harsh Reality of CRS Points

Canada's Express Entry system is one of the most sought-after immigration path for skilled workers worldwide. Express Entry operates on a points-based system known as the Comprehensive Ranking System (CRS). The CRS assigns points to applicants based on various factors, including age, education, work experience, language proficiency, and adaptability. While the system is intended to be transparent and merit-based, the harsh reality is that even highly qualified candidates often struggle to achieve the high CRS scores required to secure an Invitation to Apply (ITA) for permanent residency.

Over the years, the CRS cutoff score for Express Entry draws has remained high, often exceeding 520 points. This makes it extremely challenging for many applicants, even those with impressive qualifications, to meet the cutoff. For example, an applicant with a Master's degree, high IELTS scores (specifically 8777—8.0 in listening and 7.0 in reading, writing, and speaking), and under the age of 32 would typically score around 450 CRS points. While this would be considered a strong profile under most immigration systems, it falls short in Canada's competitive Express Entry pool, where the cutoff often surpasses 510 or even 520 points.

This creates a paradox where highly skilled, educated, and linguistically proficient candidates find themselves unable to meet the CRS cutoff despite seemingly doing everything right. The challenges of navigating the CRS system reflect the increasing competitiveness of Canada's immigration process and the need for strategic planning to enhance one's CRS score or explore alternative pathways to permanent residency.

How the CRS System Works

To understand why so many applicants struggle with CRS scores despite strong qualifications, it is essential to understand how the Comprehensive Ranking System is structured. The CRS is designed to evaluate candidates based on four primary factors: core human capital, spouse or common-law partner factors, skill transferability, and additional factors.

Core human capital factors include the applicant's age, education level, language proficiency, and Canadian work experience. Younger applicants receive higher points for age, with the maximum score awarded to those between 20 and 29 years old. Education plays a critical role in the CRS score, with higher points assigned to those holding bachelor's, master's, and doctoral degrees. Language proficiency, assessed through standardized tests such as IELTS and CELPIP, is also a major determinant of CRS points, with the highest scores awarded to those who achieve the equivalent of 3777 or higher in IELTS.

Spouse or common-law partner factors contribute additional points based on the partner's education level, language proficiency, and Canadian work experience. Skill transferability factors combine education, work experience, and language ability, rewarding applicants who demonstrate a strong mix of skills. Additional factors include having a valid job offer from a Canadian employer, a provincial nomination, or Canadian educational credentials, all of which provide significant boosts to the CRS score.

The total possible score under the CRS system is 1,200 points. However, without a provincial nomination or a valid job offer, most candidates max out at around 500 points. This means that even strong candidates who meet most of the criteria struggle to reach competitive CRS scores.

The Challenge of CRS Scores for Highly Qualified Candidates

The harsh reality for many Express Entry candidates is that meeting the basic qualifications is no longer enough to secure an ITA. In the early years of the Express Entry system, CRS cutoffs were more accessible, often falling in the range of 430 to 450 points. However, as Canada's immigration targets have shifted and the pool of applicants has become more competitive, the cutoffs have consistently remained above 470 points. A candidate with a Master's degree, high IELTS scores, and several years of work experience might expect to score between 440 and 460 points under the CRS system. While this would have been sufficient in the early years of Express Entry, recent draw thresholds have made this score insufficient for securing an ITA.

The CRS challenges are particularly difficult for single applicants. Married applicants can benefit from additional points contributed by their spouse's education, work experience, and language proficiency. Single applicants, however, are evaluated solely on their own qualifications, putting them at a disadvantage in the CRS ranking system.

Age is another critical factor that disadvantages many otherwise qualified candidates. While applicants under 30 receive the highest CRS points for age, the score begins to decrease significantly after the age of 30. By the time an applicant reaches their mid-30s, they lose valuable CRS points even if they hold a Master's degree and high IELTS scores. This creates a sense of urgency for younger applicants to maximize their CRS scores before they begin to lose points for age.

For example, a 32-year-old candidate with a Master's degree, IELTS scores of 8777, and three years of work experience might expect a CRS score of approximately 450 points. While this is a competitive profile on paper, it is unlikely to meet the cutoff unless the candidate secures additional points through a job offer, a provincial nomination, or additional language proficiency improvements. The challenge becomes even more pronounced for applicants who have limited Canadian work experience. While Canadian work experience is highly rewarded under the CRS system, international work experience receives significantly fewer points. This means that even highly skilled professionals with years of international experience find themselves at a disadvantage when competing against candidates with Canadian work history.

Why the CRS Cutoff Remains High

Several factors contribute to the consistently high CRS cutoffs in Express Entry draws. First, the volume of applications has increased significantly in recent years. Canada's reputation as a top destination for immigrants has attracted skilled professionals from around the world, increasing the level of competition within the Express Entry pool. Second, Canada's labor market has become increasingly specialized. While there is still strong demand for skilled workers, the government has placed greater emphasis on attracting immigrants who meet specific labor market needs. This has resulted in higher scores for candidates with Canadian work experience, provincial nominations, and job offers in high-demand fields such as healthcare, technology, and skilled trades.

Third, the availability of provincial nominations has reshaped the Express Entry landscape. Candidates who receive a provincial nomination are awarded an additional 600 CRS points, virtually guaranteeing an ITA. This has created a scenario where candidates with lower CRS scores can still succeed through provincial nomination programs, but those without a nomination face an uphill battle. The high CRS cutoff reflects the Canadian government's focus on selecting the most competitive and adaptable candidates. While this ensures that Canada benefits from a highly skilled immigrant workforce, it also makes it more difficult for otherwise strong candidates to succeed through Express Entry alone.

How to Overcome CRS Challenges

Despite the challenges posed by high CRS cutoffs, there are several strategies that applicants can use to improve their scores and increase their chances of receiving an ITA.

Language proficiency is one of the most influential factors under the CRS system. Even small improvements in IELTS or CELPIP scores can lead to a significant increase in CRS points. For example, achieving a CLB 10 in all language categories can add up to 50 points, which could mean the difference between receiving an ITA or missing the cutoff.

Canadian work experience is another powerful factor in boosting CRS scores. Applicants who are able to secure a temporary work permit and gain Canadian work experience can significantly improve their CRS standing. The Canadian Experience Class (CEC) under Express Entry rewards applicants with at least one year of Canadian work experience, adding valuable CRS points and increasing the likelihood of selection. Securing a provincial nomination is one of the most effective ways to overcome low CRS scores. Provincial Nominee Programs (PNPs) allow provinces and territories to nominate candidates based on local labor market needs. A provincial nomination adds 600 CRS points to an applicant's profile, virtually guaranteeing an ITA in the next draw.

Educational qualifications can also be improved to increase CRS scores. Completing a second degree or obtaining additional certifications can add points under the CRS system. For younger applicants, completing additional education before reaching the age threshold for maximum CRS points can be a strategic decision. While the challenges of the CRS system are real, strategic planning, persistence, and informed decision-making can help applicants overcome the hurdles and achieve their goal of securing Canadian permanent residency. Understanding the structure of the CRS system and adapting to the evolving requirements of Express Entry are key to turning a competitive profile into a successful application.

Sector-Specific Invitations

Canada's Express Entry system has long been recognized as one of the most structured immigration ways for workers seeking permanent residency in canada. Since its introduction in 2015, Express Entry has operated on a points-based system known as the Comprehensive Ranking System (CRS), where candidates are evaluated based on factors such as age, education, work experience, language proficiency, and adaptability. The goal of the Express Entry system is to select immigrants who have the highest potential to contribute to Canada's economy and society.

However, in recent years, the landscape of Express Entry has shifted significantly. While the CRS system initially operated as a broad merit-based ranking system where candidates from all industries and professional backgrounds competed within a single pool, the Canadian government has gradually introduced sector-specific draws to address labor shortages and meet the country's evolving economic needs. Among the most prominent trends in Express Entry draws has been the increasing focus on candidates with experience and qualifications in the healthcare sector.

This shift toward sector-specific invitations reflects the growing recognition of Canada's critical labor shortages in healthcare. Canada's aging population, combined with the increased demand for healthcare services, has created a pressing need for healthcare professionals, including doctors, nurses, medical technicians, and healthcare administrators. As a result, Express Entry draws have become increasingly tailored toward healthcare professionals, significantly boosting the chances of selection for applicants in this sector while making it more difficult for those in other fields to qualify. For applicants without healthcare experience or credentials, the rise of sector-specific draws presents a significant challenge. Even candidates with strong CRS scores, high levels of education, and impressive language proficiency may find themselves overlooked in favor of healthcare professionals who meet Canada's targeted labor market needs. This shift highlights the increasing complexity of the Canadian immigration landscape and underscores the importance of adapting one's immigration strategy to align with Canada's changing economic priorities.

Why Canada is Prioritizing Healthcare Professionals

Canada's focus on attracting healthcare professionals through Express Entry is driven by a combination of demographic and economic factors. The country's population is aging rapidly, with nearly one in five Canadians over the age of 65. This demographic shift has created a surge in demand for healthcare services, placing significant strain on Canada's healthcare infrastructure. Hospitals, long-term care facilities, and community health centers are facing staffing shortages, leading to longer wait times, reduced access to care, and increased pressure on existing healthcare professionals.

The COVID-19 pandemic further exposed the vulnerabilities in Canada's healthcare system. The sudden increase in hospitalizations and the need for specialized medical care highlighted the shortage of trained healthcare workers, particularly in rural and underserved areas. In response, the Canadian government introduced targeted measures to recruit and retain healthcare professionals, recognizing that strengthening the healthcare workforce is essential to maintaining the country's healthcare standards and ensuring public health resilience.

Immigration has long been a key strategy for addressing labor shortages in the healthcare sector. Canada's domestic supply of healthcare workers has not kept pace with demand, making it necessary to recruit internationally trained professionals. The Canadian government's decision to implement sector-specific draws targeting healthcare professionals reflects this strategic priority. By prioritizing candidates with healthcare experience, Canada aims to fill critical staffing gaps, improve access to medical care, and reduce the burden on the healthcare system.

How Sector-Specific Draws in Healthcare Work

The structure of Express Entry draws has evolved to accommodate sector-specific invitations. In a traditional Express Entry draw, candidates from all occupational backgrounds are ranked based on their CRS scores, and the highest-ranking candidates receive Invitations to Apply (ITAs) for permanent residency. However, in a sector-specific draw, the Canadian government sets aside a portion of ITAs for candidates with experience and qualifications in designated fields.

Healthcare draws typically target candidates with experience in high-demand occupations such as nursing, general medicine, pharmacy, physiotherapy, and medical technology. In some cases, the Canadian government may specify additional requirements, such as provincial licensing or proof of professional certification. Candidates who meet the criteria for healthcare sector draws are given priority, even if their overall CRS scores are lower than those of candidates in other fields. This targeted approach has resulted in lower CRS cutoffs for healthcare professionals. While general draws may have a cutoff score above 520 points, sector-specific draws for healthcare candidates have had cutoffs in the range of 350 to 400 points. This means that healthcare professionals with moderate CRS scores have a higher chance of receiving an ITA compared to highly qualified candidates in other industries.

The growing influence of sector-specific draws is evident in the data from recent Express Entry rounds. In 2023, the Canadian government conducted multiple targeted draws for healthcare professionals, issuing thousands of ITAs to candidates with experience in nursing, medical technology, and general medicine. These targeted draws accounted for a significant percentage of the total ITAs issued, reflecting the government's commitment to addressing healthcare labor shortages through immigration.

For healthcare professionals, sector-specific draws represent a significant opportunity to secure permanent residency in Canada. However, for candidates in other industries, the shift toward targeted draws has made the Express Entry process more competitive and less predictable. Candidates who would have easily qualified for permanent residency under the general CRS system now face the challenge of competing against healthcare professionals in a system that increasingly favors sector-specific experience.

The Impact on Non-Healthcare Candidates

The rise of healthcare-focused draws has created a challenging environment for candidates without experience or qualifications in the healthcare sector. Even highly skilled professionals with strong CRS scores are finding it difficult to receive ITAs due to the disproportionate allocation of invitations to healthcare candidates.

For example, an applicant with a Master's degree, high IELTS scores, and several years of work experience in the technology or financial sector might have a CRS score of around 450 points. Under normal circumstances, this would be considered a competitive score. However, if the majority of ITAs are reserved for healthcare professionals, this applicant may find themselves waiting for months, or even years, without receiving an invitation. The shift toward sector-specific draws has also affected candidates in fields that were previously considered high-demand. Technology professionals, engineers, and financial analysts, who once had high success rates through Express Entry, are now competing for fewer spots in general draws. Without additional factors such as Canadian work experience, a provincial nomination, or a job offer, these candidates face an uphill battle in securing permanent residency.

Age has become an additional barrier for non-healthcare candidates. Under the CRS system, candidates receive the highest points for age between 20 and 29 years old. After the age of 30, CRS points for age begin to decline, making it more difficult for older candidates to compete. Healthcare professionals, however, benefit from the targeted nature of sector-specific draws, which prioritize professional experience and credentials over age.

The rise of healthcare draws has also created uncertainty among non-healthcare candidates regarding the long-term stability of the Express Entry system. Immigration consultants and candidates alike have raised concerns about the fairness of targeted draws and the potential for other industries to be overlooked. While the Canadian government maintains that sector-specific draws are designed to address immediate labor market needs, the long-term impact on non-healthcare candidates remains a point of concern.

Strategies for Non-Healthcare Candidates

For non-healthcare candidates facing challenges in Express Entry, strategic planning is essential. One of the most effective strategies is securing a provincial nomination through a Provincial Nominee Program (PNP). Many provinces offer PNP streams for candidates in high-demand occupations, including technology, skilled trades, and engineering. A provincial nomination adds 600 points to a candidate's CRS score, virtually guaranteeing an ITA in the next Express Entry draw. Improving language proficiency is another powerful way to increase CRS scores. Higher IELTS or CELPIP scores can add valuable CRS points and improve a candidate's overall ranking.

Candidates who are struggling to qualify under Express Entry may also explore alternative immigration pathways, such as the Atlantic Immigration Program (AIP), the Rural and Northern Immigration Pilot (RNIP), and employer-driven programs. These pathways often have lower entry requirements and provide additional opportunities for candidates to secure permanent residency. Gaining Canadian work experience through a temporary work permit or study permit can also significantly enhance a candidate's CRS score. Canadian work experience is highly rewarded under the CRS system and can increase a candidate's competitiveness in future draws.

The rise of sector-specific draws in Express Entry reflects Canada's evolving immigration priorities and the increasing demand for healthcare professionals. While this shift has created new opportunities for healthcare candidates, it has also made the Express Entry process more challenging for non-healthcare applicants. Strategic planning, adaptability, and a thorough understanding of the CRS system are essential for navigating the complexities of Express Entry and securing permanent residency in Canada. Candidates who adjust their approach and explore alternative pathways will position themselves for long-term success in Canada's competitive immigration landscape.

Common Immigration Scams to Watch For

The complexity of Canada's immigration system, combined with the high volume of applicants, creates a vulnerable environment where scammers prey on the hopes and desperation of potential immigrants. Many of these scams are sophisticated, mimicking official government communications, legal documents, and professional websites. Scammers often promise guaranteed success, fast-tracked applications, and insider access to immigration officials, claims that are not only false but also illegal under Canadian law.

For those seeking to immigrate to Canada, awareness and vigilance are critical. Understanding the tactics used by scammers and learning how to identify red flags can help prevent falling victim to fraudulent schemes. The most common scams involve false guarantees related to Express Entry invitations, fake job offers designed to boost Comprehensive Ranking System (CRS) points, high fees for nonexistent services, and misleading claims about healthcare priorities. This chapter explores these common immigration scams in detail, providing valuable insights into how they operate and how to protect oneself from exploitation.

Guaranteed Express Entry Invitations

One of the most prevalent immigration scams targets applicants through false promises of guaranteed Express Entry invitations. The Express Entry system is one of the most competitive and transparent immigration pathways in the world. It operates on a points-based system known as the Comprehensive Ranking System (CRS), which evaluates candidates based on age, education, work experience, language proficiency, and other factors. In recent years, CRS cutoffs have remained high, often exceeding 470 points. As a result, many highly qualified candidates struggle to secure an Invitation to Apply (ITA) for permanent residency. Scammers exploit this reality by claiming to have insider access to Canadian immigration officials or direct influence over the Express Entry system. They offer to guarantee an ITA in exchange for a significant fee, often ranging from thousands to tens of thousands of dollars.

These scams typically involve a false sense of urgency. Applicants are told that they must pay immediately to secure a spot in the next draw or that a limited number of guaranteed invitations are available. Scammers may provide forged documents or fake correspondence from Immigration, Refugees and Citizenship Canada (IRCC) to make their claims more convincing. Some go as far as setting up fake websites that mimic the official Canadian government portal to trick applicants into believing they are interacting with an official agency.

The reality is that Express Entry is a strictly merit-based system. No consultant, agent, or lawyer has the power to influence CRS scores or secure an ITA outside of the official process. The CRS system operates based on a transparent algorithm that evaluates each candidate's profile according to established criteria. Invitations are issued to the highest-ranking candidates during each draw, and the results are publicly available on the IRCC website.

Despite the transparency of the Express Entry system, many applicants fall victim to scams because of the intense competition and high CRS cutoffs. Applicants who narrowly miss the cutoff or have seen their CRS scores decline due to age or other factors may feel pressured to seek alternative solutions. Scammers capitalize on this vulnerability by presenting themselves as the only viable path to success. Victims of guaranteed Express Entry scams often lose more than just money. In some cases, scammers advise applicants to falsify information on their Express Entry profiles or provide fake documents to increase their CRS scores. Submitting false information to IRCC is a serious offense that can result in a five-year ban from applying for Canadian immigration. Even if the scam is discovered after the applicant has already been granted permanent residency, IRCC has the authority to revoke their status and initiate deportation proceedings.

Applicants should remain cautious of any consultant or agency that claims to guarantee an ITA or fast-track the Express Entry process. Legitimate immigration consultants, who are registered with the College of Immigration and Citizenship Consultants (CICC), are prohibited from making such claims under Canadian law. Any promise of guaranteed success should be treated as a red flag.

Fake Job Offers to Boost Points

Job offers from Canadian employers are highly valuable under the CRS system. An arranged employment offer can add up to 200 CRS points to an applicant's profile, significantly improving their chances of securing an ITA. Given the competitive nature of Express Entry draws, many applicants view securing a job offer as the key to success. Scammers have capitalized on this demand by creating a sophisticated network of fake job offers designed to deceive unsuspecting applicants. Fake job offer scams often begin with an unsolicited email or social media message from a supposed Canadian employer or recruitment agency. The offer is presented as a high-paying job in a desirable location, often in industries where labor shortages exist, such as healthcare, construction, and information technology. The scammer may provide a detailed job description, employment contract, and even a letter of support for the applicant's work permit or immigration application.

The catch is that the applicant is required to pay a "processing fee" or "employment bond" to secure the job. This fee can range from a few hundred to several thousand dollars. In some cases, the scammer may request sensitive personal information, such as passport details, social insurance numbers, and bank account information, under the guise of processing the employment contract. After the payment is made, the job offer either disappears entirely, or the applicant is informed that additional fees are required to complete the process. In other cases, the applicant may arrive in Canada only to discover that the job does not exist, leaving them financially and emotionally devastated.

Fake job offers are particularly dangerous because they often involve forged documents that appear legitimate. Some scammers even create fake websites for non-existent companies or impersonate real Canadian businesses. Applicants who unknowingly submit fake job offers to IRCC as part of their immigration application risk having their application denied and facing a ban for misrepresentation.

To avoid falling victim to fake job offer scams, applicants should verify the legitimacy of the employer and the job offer. IRCC maintains a list of approved employers for the Temporary Foreign Worker Program (TFWP) and the International Mobility Program (IMP). Applicants should also contact the employer directly using official contact information listed on the company's website. Any request for payment in exchange for a job offer should be treated as a red flag, as Canadian labor laws prohibit employers from charging fees to prospective employees.

High Fees for Nonexistent Services

Another common immigration scam involves charging excessively high fees for nonexistent or unnecessary services. Some fraudulent consultants and agencies claim to provide special access to immigration programs, exclusive legal advice, or fast-tracked application processing. These services are often marketed with professional-looking websites, client testimonials, and high-pressure sales tactics designed to create a sense of urgency.

Applicants are often asked to pay large upfront fees before receiving any tangible service. In some cases, the consultant may disappear after receiving the payment, leaving the applicant without any support or guidance. In other cases, the consultant may provide incorrect advice, submit incomplete applications, or fail to meet deadlines, leading to the rejection of the immigration application. Applicants should be cautious of any consultant who demands full payment upfront or charges significantly higher fees than the industry standard. Licensed immigration consultants, who are registered with the CICC, are required to follow strict guidelines regarding fee structures and payment terms. Applicants should request a detailed contract that outlines the scope of services, payment terms, and refund policies before engaging the services of a consultant.

Unrealistic Claims About Healthcare Priority

Healthcare professionals are in high demand in Canada, and the Canadian government has introduced targeted Express Entry draws to recruit skilled healthcare workers. However, some fraudulent consultants mislead non-healthcare applicants by claiming that they can secure invitations under healthcare-specific draws even if the applicant does not meet the requirements.

Some scammers offer to provide fake healthcare credentials or fabricated work experience to increase an applicant's CRS score. This type of fraud is highly risky, as IRCC conducts thorough background checks and verification processes. Submitting false information to IRCC can result in application denial, permanent bans, and legal consequences. Applicants should only apply for sector-specific draws if they meet the official requirements set by IRCC. Claims of being able to bypass these requirements should be treated as a red flag

Immigrating to Canada is a structured and highly regulated process. While the complexity of the system can create challenges, there are no shortcuts or guaranteed outcomes. Scammers prey on desperation and uncertainty, offering false promises that lead to financial loss and legal consequences. Understanding the structure of Canada's immigration system and relying on licensed professionals are the best ways to avoid falling victim to scams. Applicants who remain informed and vigilant will position themselves for long-term success in their Canadian immigration journey.

Bridging the Gap: Realistic Steps to Improve Your CRS Score

The promise of a better life, a stable economy, world-class healthcare, and a thriving multicultural society makes Canada one of the most desirable immigration destinations. However, the journey to Canadian permanent residency is not always smooth, particularly for those navigating the complexities of the Express Entry system.

Canada's Express Entry system is designed to select skilled workers based on a merit-based points system known as the Comprehensive Ranking System (CRS). The CRS assigns points based on several factors, including age, education, language proficiency, work experience, and adaptability. Applicants with the highest CRS scores are invited to apply for permanent residency during regular Express Entry draws. While the system is intended to be fair and transparent, the reality is that CRS cutoffs have remained consistently high, often exceeding 470 points. For many qualified candidates, achieving a competitive CRS score is an uphill battle. Even individuals with impressive credentials, a Master's degree, high IELTS scores (8777), and several years of work experience, find themselves falling short of the CRS cutoff. This creates a gap between the qualifications of the applicant and the requirements of the system, making it difficult to secure an Invitation to Apply (ITA) for permanent residency.

Faced with this challenge, some applicants fall into the trap of immigration scams. Fraudulent agents and consultants exploit the pressure and desperation felt by applicants, offering false promises of guaranteed Express Entry invitations, fake job offers, and insider access to Canadian immigration officials. These scams not only drain applicants of their money but also jeopardize their chances of ever securing Canadian residency due to potential misrepresentation or fraud.

Instead of falling prey to these fraudulent schemes, applicants can focus on strategic and legitimate methods to bridge the gap in their CRS score. The key to success lies in understanding the structure of the CRS system and identifying areas where additional points can be gained. Enhancing one's credentials, exploring Provincial Nominee Programs (PNPs), considering alternative immigration pathways, and seeking genuine expert advice are some of the most effective strategies to increase CRS scores and improve the chances of receiving an ITA.

Enhance Your Credentials

One of the most effective ways to increase a CRS score is by improving one's qualifications and credentials. The CRS system is designed to reward candidates with high levels of education, strong language proficiency, and relevant work experience. Enhancing any of these factors can lead to a significant increase in points and improve the applicant's position in the Express Entry pool. Education plays a critical role in the CRS system. Higher levels of education are rewarded with more points, and the combination of a Canadian degree or diploma with foreign education can lead to even higher scores. For example, a candidate with a bachelor's degree from their home country can significantly increase their CRS score by completing a postgraduate diploma or master's degree in Canada. Studying in Canada not only boosts CRS points but also provides the added benefit of Canadian educational credentials, which are highly valued in the labor market and increase the chances of securing a job offer.

Language proficiency is another powerful factor in the CRS calculation. The Canadian Language Benchmark (CLB) measures language proficiency in four categories, reading, writing, speaking, and listening. Applicants who achieve high CLB scores, particularly CLB 9 or higher, receive significant CRS points. For instance, improving an IELTS score from CLB 8 to CLB 9 can add up to 50 points to the CRS score. Even small improvements in individual language test scores can make a substantial difference in the overall CRS ranking.

For many applicants, the most practical way to increase language proficiency is through focused preparation and retesting. Enrolling in professional language training programs, working with a language coach, and practicing consistently can lead to measurable improvements in test performance. Since language proficiency is one of the most heavily weighted factors in the CRS system, maximizing points in this category is essential. Work experience is another area where CRS scores can be enhanced. While Canadian work experience is valued more highly than foreign experience under the CRS system, increasing overall work experience still adds valuable points. For example, a candidate with three years of foreign work experience will receive more CRS points than a candidate with only one year of experience. Candidates who are below the CRS cutoff may benefit from gaining additional work experience before reapplying.

Canadian work experience carries even more weight under the CRS system. Candidates who have the opportunity to work in Canada through a temporary work permit or an employer-sponsored visa can significantly boost their CRS scores. Programs such as the Temporary Foreign Worker Program (TFWP) and the International Mobility Program (IMP) provide avenues for securing Canadian work experience, which not only increases CRS points but also improves the chances of obtaining a job offer.

Educational credentials, language proficiency, and work experience are the foundation of a strong CRS score. Candidates who strategically invest in improving these areas place themselves in a better position to meet or exceed the CRS cutoff and secure an ITA through Express Entry.

Explore Provincial Nominee Programs (PNPs)

For candidates who struggle to reach competitive CRS scores through the Express Entry pool alone, Provincial Nominee Programs (PNPs) offer a powerful alternative. PNPs allow Canadian provinces and territories to select candidates based on their specific labor market needs and economic priorities. A provincial nomination adds 600 CRS points to an applicant's profile, virtually guaranteeing an ITA in the next Express Entry draw.

Each province in Canada has its own PNP, with unique criteria and target occupations. Some provinces prioritize healthcare professionals, while others focus on technology workers, skilled trades, or agricultural labor. The key to success through PNPs lies in identifying provinces with labor shortages or economic demands that align with the candidate's skills and qualifications. Ontario, British Columbia, and Alberta have some of the largest and most active PNPs. Ontario's Human Capital Priorities Stream, for example, regularly issues invitations to candidates with high-demand skills in the technology, healthcare, and finance sectors. British Columbia's Tech Pilot targets candidates with experience in technology fields such as software development, artificial intelligence, and cybersecurity.

Even candidates with CRS scores as low as 300 to 400 points can receive an ITA through a provincial nomination. This makes PNPs an attractive option for candidates who struggle to reach the competitive CRS cutoffs in general Express Entry draws.

Applying for a PNP requires a strategic approach. Candidates must demonstrate that they meet the specific requirements of the province, including language proficiency, work experience, and adaptability factors. Some PNPs require candidates to have a valid job offer from an employer in the province, while others accept applications from candidates with transferable skills and education.

Consider Alternative Pathways

While Express Entry remains the most popular immigration way to Canada, several alternative programs offer opportunities for candidates who face challenges in meeting CRS cutoffs. The Atlantic Immigration Program (AIP) and the Rural and Northern Immigration Pilot (RNIP) are two such programs designed to attract skilled workers to smaller communities and less populated regions of Canada. The Atlantic Immigration Program targets skilled workers and international graduates who are willing to settle in one of Canada's four Atlantic provinces; New Brunswick, Nova Scotia, Prince Edward Island, and Newfoundland and Labrador. The program is employer-driven, meaning that candidates must secure a job offer from an approved employer in the Atlantic region. Successful applicants receive permanent residency and are encouraged to establish long-term roots in the region.

The Rural and Northern Immigration Pilot is designed to address labor shortages in smaller communities across Canada. Candidates who secure job offers in designated rural and northern communities receive support from local governments and businesses to integrate into the community and establish themselves economically. These alternative pathways often have lower entry requirements than Express Entry and provide candidates with an opportunity to secure permanent residency without the pressure of competing against the CRS system's high cutoffs.

Seek Genuine Expert Advice

Navigating the complexities of Canadian immigration requires expert guidance. Many candidates turn to immigration consultants and lawyers for support, but not all professionals are qualified or trustworthy. It is essential to work with licensed professionals who are registered with the College of Immigration and Citizenship Consultants (CICC) or provincial law societies. An experienced immigration consultant can help candidates identify weaknesses in their profile, develop strategies to improve CRS scores, and explore alternative immigration pathways. Genuine experts provide realistic advice, manage the application process efficiently, and ensure that all documentation is accurate and complete.

Bridging the gap in CRS scores requires a strategic, informed, and long-term approach. Enhancing educational credentials, improving language proficiency, gaining Canadian work experience, and exploring provincial nominations are the most effective ways to increase CRS points. Candidates who invest in these areas and seek expert guidance position themselves for success in Canada's competitive immigration landscape. By focusing on legitimate strategies and avoiding shortcuts, candidates can achieve their Canadian dream with confidence and integrity.

Author's Insight: Don't be misled by flashy ads or promotional videos from large immigration firms that push Express Entry as a one-size-fits-all solution. Always calculate your CRS score independently to assess where you truly stand, estimate your IELTS score based on your actual language proficiency. If your CRS score is close to 510–520, you can confidently proceed with Express Entry, whether through a certified agent or immigration lawyer.

However, if your score is around 440–450, it's wise to explore alternative pathways such as the study route, Provincial Nominee Program (PNP), Start-Up Visa, or investment-based options.

Avoid falling for fraudulent LMIA-based job offers. Instead, focus on seeking legitimate employment opportunities through trusted job portals, though it's important to acknowledge that securing a job offer from abroad can be challenging.

Chapter - 4

Immigration Then and Now: Comparing Immigration Over Two Decades

Canada has long been known as a land of opportunity for immigrants seeking a better future. Over the past two decades, the Canadian immigration landscape has undergone profound changes, reflecting the country's shifting economic needs, political priorities, and global trends. From evolving immigration policies to changing demographic patterns and labor market demands, the pathway to Canadian permanent residency has become increasingly complex and competitive. For many years, Canada's reputation as a welcoming and diverse nation has made it one of the most sought-after destinations for immigrants. However, the process of gaining entry and establishing permanent residency has not remained static. Immigration policies that were once focused on family reunification and humanitarian grounds have gradually shifted toward a more skills-based approach, aimed at attracting highly educated and skilled professionals who can contribute to Canada's economy.

This transformation has been driven by several key factors, including labor shortages, an aging population, and the rise of global competition for talent. While Canada remains committed to its core values of diversity and inclusion, the increasing emphasis on economic immigration has created new challenges for prospective immigrants. Today, securing permanent residency requires not only meeting basic eligibility criteria but also excelling in a competitive points-based system and, in some cases, adapting to sector-specific demands. The evolution of Canada's immigration system over the past two decades reflects the changing nature of global mobility and the strategic role that immigration plays in shaping the country's future. By comparing the immigration landscape of the early 2000s with the current system, it becomes clear that the path to Canadian residency has become more structured, merit-based, and tailored to the country's labor market needs. Understanding these changes provides valuable insights for prospective immigrants seeking to navigate Canada's modern immigration system.

The LMIA Conundrum: Missing Points in Express Entry

The Canada's structured immigration policies, combined with its strong labor market and open social fabric, have made it a global leader in attracting top talent from around the world. One of the key pathways for skilled workers to enter Canada has been through the Labour Market Impact Assessment (LMIA) process, which allows Canadian employers to hire foreign workers when they cannot find suitable candidates within the domestic labor force.

Holding an LMIA-based work permit was considered a golden ticket for gaining Canadian permanent residency. Under the old immigration system, securing an LMIA was seen as a direct route to accumulating the necessary points under the Comprehensive Ranking System (CRS) and securing an Invitation to Apply (ITA) for permanent residency under the Express Entry system. LMIA-based job offers were awarded high CRS points, giving LMIA holders a significant advantage over other applicants in the Express Entry pool. However, in recent years, the Canadian government has introduced significant changes to the LMIA policy and its relationship to the Express Entry system. These changes have made it more difficult for LMIA holders to leverage their work permits to gain permanent residency. The number of CRS points awarded for an LMIA-based job offer has been reduced significantly, and the eligibility requirements for LMIA processing have become more complex and restrictive.

As a result, many LMIA holders now face uncertainty and frustration in their transition to permanent residency, while Canadian employers struggle to retain skilled talent who may seek alternative pathways. The LMIA conundrum represents a critical challenge for both foreign workers and Canadian employers. Understanding the impact of LMIA policy changes and exploring strategic solutions is essential for navigating Canada's evolving immigration landscape and securing long-term residency and career stability.

The Impact of LMIA Policy Changes

The landscape changed dramatically in 2016 when the Canadian government introduced significant changes to the CRS points system for LMIA-based job offers under Express Entry. The number of CRS points awarded for a valid job offer backed by an LMIA was reduced from 600 points to between 50 and 200 points, depending on the type of job. High-skilled positions listed under the National Occupational Classification (NOC) at levels 0, A, and B were reduced to 50 points. Only senior managerial positions at NOC level 00 continued to receive 200 points. This marked a significant reduction in the value of LMIA-based job offers in the Express Entry system, making it more difficult for LMIA holders to reach the competitive CRS cutoffs required to secure an ITA.

The policy change reflected the Canadian government's shift toward a more comprehensive and balanced approach to economic immigration. The government sought to prevent over-reliance on job offers and ensure that the selection process remained focused on overall human capital factors, including education, language proficiency, and work experience. The intention was to create a level playing field for applicants and reduce the disproportionate advantage that LMIA holders had enjoyed under the previous system. While the policy changes were designed to promote fairness and balance within the Express Entry pool, they created unintended consequences for LMIA holders. Many foreign workers who had secured LMIA-based work permits with the expectation of gaining permanent residency found themselves at a disadvantage when their CRS scores were no longer high enough to meet the cutoffs.

For example, a candidate with a Master's degree, high IELTS scores (8777), and several years of work experience might have scored around 450 points under the CRS system. Before the policy changes, a positive LMIA would have added 600 points, boosting the total score to over 1,000 and virtually guaranteeing an ITA. After the policy changes, the same LMIA would only add 50 points, raising the score to 500—still competitive but no longer a guaranteed path to residency, particularly in draws where cutoffs exceed 470 or 480 points.

This created a situation where LMIA holders with strong profiles but without a provincial nomination or Canadian work experience faced significant challenges in securing permanent residency. The reduction in CRS points awarded for LMIA-based job offers also affected employers, who now struggled to retain skilled workers whose immigration status had become uncertain.

Challenges Faced by LMIA Holders

The reduction in CRS points for LMIA-based job offers has had a cascading effect on LMIA holders and their employers. Many LMIA holders who were previously on track for permanent residency now face the risk of losing their legal status in Canada once their work permits expire.

The Express Entry system operates on a dynamic points-based ranking, where CRS cutoffs are determined by the pool of applicants and the government's annual immigration targets. High CRS cutoffs in recent years have made it more difficult for LMIA holders to qualify, even with a valid job offer. LMIA holders who are unable to secure permanent residency through Express Entry face the difficult choice of either leaving Canada or exploring alternative immigration pathways, such as the Provincial Nominee Program (PNP). However, PNPs often have their own eligibility criteria and application timelines, making them less accessible to some applicants.

Employers are also facing challenges in retaining skilled talent. LMIA-based hires were once viewed as a reliable solution to labor shortages, providing employers with a clear mechanism for securing long-term workforce stability. However, the uncertainty surrounding permanent residency for LMIA holders has led to increased turnover and higher recruitment costs. Some LMIA holders are choosing to leave Canada for other destinations where immigration policies are more favorable, further exacerbating labor shortages in critical sectors.

Strategic Solutions for LMIA Holders and Employers

To overcome the challenges created by LMIA policy changes, both foreign workers and Canadian employers must adopt strategic approaches to securing permanent residency and workforce retention. One effective solution is to combine LMIA-based job offers with provincial nominations. PNPs allow provinces to nominate candidates based on local labor market needs. Securing a provincial nomination adds 600 CRS points to an applicant's profile, virtually guaranteeing an ITA in the next Express Entry draw.

Employers can also explore employer-driven immigration programs such as the Atlantic Immigration Program (AIP) and the Rural and Northern Immigration Pilot (RNIP). These programs provide alternative pathways to permanent residency for skilled workers and help employers address labor shortages in specific regions. Improving language proficiency, gaining additional work experience, and completing additional educational credentials are other effective strategies for increasing CRS scores.

Filling the Gap: Strategies for Success

Immigrating to Canada has become increasingly competitive in recent years. With rising Comprehensive Ranking System (CRS) cutoffs, changing immigration policies, and sector-specific draws, securing permanent residency is no longer a straightforward process. For many skilled professionals, entrepreneurs, and business owners, the path to Canadian residency is complicated by high CRS score requirements, shifting labor market priorities, and new immigration targets focused on healthcare and technology sectors. Despite these challenges, Canada remains one of the most attractive destinations for immigrants worldwide due to its high standard of living, political stability, economic opportunities, and welcoming social environment.

For many applicants, the gap between their current CRS score and the required cutoff has become the single biggest obstacle to securing an Invitation to Apply (ITA) through the Express Entry system. Applicants with high levels of education, significant work experience, and strong language proficiency are still finding themselves falling short of the required CRS scores due to increasing competition in the Express Entry pool. Furthermore, changes to the Labour Market Impact Assessment (LMIA) policy have made it more difficult for LMIA holders to leverage their work permits to gain permanent residency. This creates a situation where many skilled workers face uncertainty about their future status in Canada despite contributing to the economy and filling critical labor market gaps.

To overcome these challenges, both applicants and employers need to adopt innovative and strategic approaches to bridge the gap and achieve their immigration goals. Canada's immigration system remains dynamic, with new programs, alternative pathways, and strategic opportunities emerging to address labor shortages and attract skilled talent. By understanding the structure of the Canadian immigration system and exploring alternative routes, applicants can position themselves for success and increase their chances of securing permanent residency. Leveraging alternative programs, improving skills and certifications, exploring family and investment pathways, and securing provincial nominations are among the most effective strategies for overcoming the barriers to permanent residency.

Leveraging Alternative Programs

As the Express Entry system becomes more competitive, alternative immigration programs have emerged as valuable tools for applicants seeking to secure Canadian residency. The Canadian government has introduced several targeted programs designed to address specific labor market gaps and support the economic growth of smaller regions. These alternative programs often have lower eligibility thresholds and provide applicants with more flexibility than the general Express Entry system. One of the most attractive alternative programs is the Start-Up Visa program, which allows entrepreneurs and business owners to obtain permanent residency by launching an innovative business in Canada.

The Start-Up Visa program is designed to attract business-minded immigrants who have the potential to create jobs and drive economic growth. To qualify, applicants must secure the backing of a designated Canadian venture capital fund, angel investor group, or business incubator. Unlike the Express Entry system, which is based on CRS scores, the Start-Up Visa program focuses on the strength and viability of the business idea.

The Start-Up Visa program offers several advantages for business owners and entrepreneurs. Successful applicants are granted permanent residency even before the business becomes fully operational, providing them with long-term stability and security. Additionally, business owners who participate in the program gain access to Canada's strong business network, government funding opportunities, and a skilled labor market. The Canadian government actively supports business development through tax incentives, research grants, and access to capital, making it easier for entrepreneurs to scale their businesses and contribute to the economy. Provincial Nominee Programs (PNPs) have also become an essential strategy for bridging the CRS gap. PNPs allow Canadian provinces and territories to select candidates based on local labor market needs and economic priorities. Each province has its own set of PNP streams, which target specific industries and professional backgrounds. For example, Ontario's Human Capital Priorities Stream focuses on technology and healthcare professionals, while British Columbia's Tech Pilot targets candidates with experience in software development, artificial intelligence, and cybersecurity.

Securing a provincial nomination adds 600 CRS points to an applicant's profile, virtually guaranteeing an ITA in the next Express Entry draw. This makes PNPs one of the most powerful tools for applicants with lower CRS scores who are struggling to qualify under the general Express Entry system. Some PNPs have specific streams designed for LMIA holders, allowing foreign workers with valid job offers to receive additional points and improve their chances of securing permanent residency. The Rural and Northern Immigration Pilot (RNIP) and the Atlantic Immigration Program (AIP) are two additional programs that offer alternative pathways to permanent residency. The RNIP targets smaller communities and rural areas that face labor shortages and population decline. Applicants who secure a job offer in one of the designated communities can apply for permanent residency through the RNIP, even if their CRS scores are below the national average. The program provides additional support for newcomers, including settlement services and access to local networks, making it easier for applicants to integrate into the community and build a stable future.

The Atlantic Immigration Program (AIP) focuses on the four Atlantic provinces: New Brunswick, Nova Scotia, Prince Edward Island, and Newfoundland and Labrador. The AIP allows employers in these provinces to hire foreign workers without the need for an LMIA, streamlining the hiring process and reducing the administrative burden for employers. Successful applicants under the AIP receive permanent residency and are encouraged to settle in the Atlantic region, where they can benefit from a lower cost of living, a strong sense of community, and growing economic opportunities.

Exploring these alternative programs requires a strategic approach. Applicants must carefully evaluate their qualifications, career goals, and settlement preferences to identify the most suitable program. Working with a licensed immigration consultant or lawyer can help applicants navigate the application process and maximize their chances of success.

Skill Development and Certification

Improving one's skill set and obtaining professional certification are powerful strategies for increasing CRS scores and enhancing competitiveness in the Express Entry pool. The CRS system places a strong emphasis on human capital factors such as education, work experience, and language proficiency. By investing in skill development and certification, applicants can increase their CRS scores and improve their overall profile.

Language proficiency is one of the most heavily weighted factors in the CRS system. The Canadian Language Benchmark (CLB) measures language proficiency in reading, writing, speaking, and listening. Applicants who achieve CLB 9 or higher receive significant CRS points, improving their chances of securing an ITA. Professional language training programs, practice tests, and targeted study plans can help applicants improve their language scores and maximize their CRS points.

Educational qualifications also play a critical role in the CRS system. Higher levels of education are rewarded with more points, and Canadian educational credentials are particularly valuable. Applicants who complete a diploma, degree, or certification program in Canada receive additional CRS points and improve their competitiveness in the job market. Professional certification in fields such as healthcare, technology, and skilled trades can also increase an applicant's chances of securing a job offer and a provincial nomination. Gaining additional work experience is another effective way to increase CRS scores. Canadian work experience is highly valued under the CRS system and provides a significant boost to an applicant's profile. Securing a temporary work permit through the International Mobility Program (IMP) or the Temporary Foreign Worker Program (TFWP) allows applicants to gain valuable Canadian work experience and improve their CRS ranking.

Exploring Family and Investment Pathways

Family sponsorship and investment-based immigration programs provide additional opportunities for applicants to secure permanent residency. Canada's family sponsorship program allows Canadian citizens and permanent residents to sponsor spouses, children, parents, and grandparents for permanent residency. While family sponsorship programs have their own eligibility requirements and processing timelines, they provide a valuable alternative for applicants who may not qualify under the Express Entry system.

Investment-based immigration programs, such as the Quebec Immigrant Investor Program (QIIP), offer permanent residency to high-net-worth individuals who make a significant financial investment in Canada's economy. The QIIP requires applicants to invest at least CAD $1.2 million in a government-approved investment fund. Successful applicants receive permanent residency and are encouraged to establish business operations in Quebec.

Chapter - 5

Booming Sectors, Big Rewards: Careers That Pay in Canada

Canada has established itself as one of the most promising destinations for skilled professionals, entrepreneurs, and business owners looking to build rewarding careers. With a stable economy, a transparent legal framework, and a high standard of living, Canada has become a magnet for ambitious individuals seeking both financial success and personal fulfillment. Over the past two decades, Canada's labor market has evolved significantly, with certain sectors experiencing remarkable growth and offering lucrative opportunities for skilled workers. The Canadian government's strategic approach to immigration reflects the country's need for talent in these booming sectors. Canada's immigration system, particularly the Express Entry program and the Provincial Nominee Programs (PNPs), prioritizes candidates with experience and qualifications in high-demand industries. As a result, professionals in these sectors not only have a better chance of securing permanent residency but also stand to benefit from competitive salaries, job stability, and career advancement opportunities.

For students, skilled professionals, and entrepreneurs considering a move to Canada, understanding the most profitable and in-demand sectors is essential for making informed career decisions. The sectors that offer the highest salaries and strongest job prospects are typically those aligned with Canada's long-term economic priorities, technological advancements, and demographic needs. Industries such as technology, healthcare, finance, natural resources, and skilled trades are among the fastest-growing and highest-paying in the country. Pursuing a career in one of these booming sectors not only increases the likelihood of securing permanent residency but also offers the potential for long-term financial security and professional growth. By understanding the dynamics of Canada's labor market and aligning one's career goals with the country's economic priorities, immigrants can maximize their earning potential and establish themselves as valuable contributors to the Canadian economy.

Top Career Fields in the Management Sector

Canada's management sector has emerged as one of the most rewarding and sought-after fields for professionals seeking high salaries, career advancement, and long-term job security. With its stable economy, thriving business environment, and increasing focus on technological innovation and global trade, Canada has become a prime destination for management professionals from around the world. The demand for skilled managers has grown steadily over the past decade, driven by the expansion of multinational corporations, the rise of digital businesses, and the increasing complexity of business operations in a globalized economy.

Management is a broad and diverse field that encompasses various industries and specializations, including digital marketing, business analytics, project management, and finance. The Canadian government recognizes the critical role that management professionals play in driving economic growth and ensuring business competitiveness. As a result, management professionals are highly valued under the Express Entry system, the Provincial Nominee Programs (PNPs), and employer-sponsored immigration pathways. For immigrants seeking to establish themselves in Canada's business landscape, a career in the management sector offers not only financial rewards but also opportunities for leadership, strategic influence, and professional development. High salaries, competitive benefits, and career progression opportunities make management one of the most attractive career fields in Canada. Furthermore, the growing integration of technology and business strategy has created new opportunities for management professionals with expertise in digital transformation, data analysis, and global market expansion.

Digital Marketing

The rise of digital business and online commerce has transformed the marketing industry, creating a high demand for professionals with expertise in digital marketing. As businesses shift from traditional advertising to digital platforms, the need for strategic marketing managers who can navigate the complexities of online consumer behavior, social media trends, and search engine algorithms has increased dramatically.

Digital marketing has become one of the fastest-growing segments within the management sector, with Canadian businesses investing heavily in online presence, brand positioning, and customer engagement. Companies in industries such as retail, technology, finance, and healthcare have recognized the power of digital marketing in driving customer acquisition and revenue growth. The average salary for a digital marketing manager in Canada ranges from CAD $70,000 to $120,000 per year, with senior-level positions commanding salaries exceeding CAD $150,000. Professionals with expertise in search engine optimization (SEO), pay-per-click (PPC) advertising, and social media strategy are particularly in demand.

E-commerce has been a major driver of growth in the digital marketing sector. The shift toward online shopping has created new opportunities for marketing professionals who understand customer behavior in digital environments and can optimize conversion rates through data-driven strategies. Companies like Shopify, Amazon, and Canadian Tire have built strong e-commerce platforms, creating consistent demand for digital marketing managers with experience in online retail and customer experience management.

Digital marketing professionals with specialized certifications, such as Google Ads, Facebook Blueprint, and HubSpot Inbound Marketing, are highly valued by Canadian employers. These certifications demonstrate a candidate's technical proficiency and strategic understanding of digital platforms, increasing their competitiveness in the job market..

Business Analytics

Business analytics has become one of the most influential fields in the management sector, as companies increasingly rely on data to inform strategic decision-making. The rise of big data, cloud computing, and predictive modeling has created a surge in demand for business analysts who can interpret complex data sets and translate them into actionable business strategies. Business analysts play a critical role in helping companies improve operational efficiency, enhance customer experience, and identify new market opportunities. They collect and analyze data from various sources, including sales reports, customer feedback, financial statements, and market research. Using statistical models and data visualization tools, business analysts uncover patterns, trends, and insights that enable executives to make informed decisions.

The demand for business analysts in Canada spans across industries, including finance, healthcare, retail, and technology. Major corporations such as RBC, Bell Canada, and Air Canada have established large data analytics teams to support business strategy and operational performance. Business analysts are also in high demand within Canada's growing startup ecosystem, where data-driven decision-making is critical for scaling operations and securing venture capital funding. The average salary for a business analyst in Canada ranges from CAD $70,000 to $120,000, with senior-level positions reaching upwards of CAD $150,000. Business analysts with specialized skills in machine learning, artificial intelligence, and data visualization tools such as Tableau and Power BI are highly sought after.

MBA Graduates

An MBA remains one of the most valuable and versatile degrees in the management sector. Canadian businesses place a high value on MBA graduates for their strategic thinking, leadership skills, and financial acumen. An MBA opens doors to senior management positions across industries, including finance, consulting, healthcare, and technology. MBA graduates are often recruited into management trainee programs, corporate strategy roles, and executive leadership positions. Companies such as Deloitte, McKinsey, and TD Bank have established dedicated recruitment channels for MBA graduates from top Canadian and international business schools.

The average starting salary for MBA graduates in Canada ranges from CAD $90,000 to $120,000, with senior executives and directors earning upwards of CAD $200,000. MBA graduates with specialized concentrations in finance, marketing, operations, and technology are particularly in demand. The rise of entrepreneurship and venture capital funding has also created opportunities for MBA graduates to launch their own businesses or secure funding for innovative projects. Canada's startup ecosystem provides a supportive environment for MBA graduates with entrepreneurial ambitions, including access to incubators, accelerators, and angel investor networks.

Project Management

Project management has become one of the most essential functions in modern business operations. Companies rely on project managers to oversee complex initiatives, ensure timely delivery, and manage budgets and resources effectively. Project management is particularly critical in industries such as construction, information technology, healthcare, and infrastructure. The average salary for a project manager in Canada ranges from CAD $80,000 to $120,000, with senior project managers earning upwards of CAD $150,000. Certifications such as Project Management Professional (PMP) and Certified ScrumMaster (CSM) are highly valued by Canadian employers and often lead to higher compensation and career advancement opportunities.

Management Consulting

Management consultants are hired by businesses to solve strategic challenges, improve operational efficiency, and enhance profitability. Top consulting firms, including McKinsey, Bain & Company, and Boston Consulting Group, have a strong presence in Canada, offering high-paying roles for experienced professionals. Management consultants earn between CAD $90,000 and $150,000 per year, with partners and senior executives earning well over CAD $200,000.

Specialized consulting in fields such as technology, healthcare, and sustainability is in particularly high demand.

Finance

The finance sector in Canada offers a wide range of high-demand careers that provide excellent earning potential, career progression, and professional development opportunities. Financial managers, investment bankers, portfolio managers, risk analysts, and financial advisors are among the most sought-after professionals in the industry. Financial management is one of the highest-paying fields in the finance sector. Financial managers are responsible for overseeing the financial health of an organization, including budgeting, financial reporting, investment strategy, and risk management. In large corporations, financial managers work closely with senior executives to develop long-term financial plans and improve operational efficiency. Salaries for financial managers range from CAD $90,000 to $150,000 annually, with senior managers and directors earning over CAD $200,000. Investment banking remains one of the most competitive and lucrative fields within the finance sector. Investment bankers provide strategic advisory services to corporate clients, including capital raising, mergers and acquisitions, and market entry strategies. Analysts and associates typically start with salaries in the range of CAD $80,000 to $120,000, with substantial bonuses based on performance. Managing directors and senior partners in investment banking can earn total compensation packages exceeding CAD $500,000, including performance-based incentives.

Financial advisory and wealth management offer attractive career opportunities for professionals with strong interpersonal and analytical skills. Financial advisors work with clients to develop customized financial plans, including investment strategies, retirement planning, and tax optimization. Salaries for financial advisors range from CAD $60,000 to $120,000, with top performers earning commissions and bonuses based on assets under management (AUM). Senior wealth managers who oversee high-net-worth client portfolios can earn over CAD $300,000 annually.

Top Career Fields in the IT Sector

The Information Technology (IT) sector in Canada has emerged as one of the most dynamic and rapidly growing industries in the world. Canada's strategic focus on technological advancement, combined with a highly skilled workforce and government-backed support for innovation, has positioned the country as a global leader in IT. Over the past two decades, Canada's IT sector has expanded at an unprecedented pace, creating high-paying jobs, fostering innovation, and attracting talent from around the world. Cities such as Toronto, Vancouver, Montreal, and Ottawa have become major technology hubs, attracting global tech giants like Google, Amazon, Microsoft, and IBM, as well as nurturing a thriving ecosystem of homegrown startups. Canada's competitive edge in the IT sector stems from its commitment to research and development (R&D), investment in digital infrastructure, and a business-friendly regulatory environment. The rise of cloud computing, artificial intelligence (AI), big data, cybersecurity, and data analytics has fueled demand for skilled professionals, making IT one of the most sought-after and rewarding career fields in Canada.

Artificial Intelligence (AI)

Artificial intelligence (AI) is revolutionizing industries globally, and Canada is at the forefront of this technological wave. Canada's strategic investment in AI research and development has positioned the country as a global leader in machine learning, natural language processing, computer vision, and robotics. Toronto has become one of the leading AI hubs in the world, home to the Vector Institute for Artificial Intelligence, which conducts cutting-edge research and attracts top talent from around the globe. The demand for AI talent in Canada has outpaced the supply, creating a highly competitive job market for skilled professionals. Machine learning engineers, AI researchers, and data scientists are among the highest-paid professionals in the tech sector, with salaries ranging from CAD $100,000 to $180,000 per year. Senior AI engineers and research scientists can command salaries exceeding CAD $200,000, with additional bonuses and stock options in high-growth startups and multinational corporations.

The Canadian government has supported AI development through initiatives such as the Pan-Canadian Artificial Intelligence Strategy, which allocated CAD $125 million to strengthen AI research and talent development. The strategy aims to create an ecosystem where AI innovation thrives, supported by academic research, industry partnerships, and government funding. For immigrants and international students with expertise in AI, Canada offers an ideal environment to build a successful career. The Global Talent Stream, part of Canada's Temporary Foreign Worker Program (TFWP), allows Canadian tech companies to fast-track the hiring of AI professionals, reducing visa processing times to as little as two weeks. This streamlined process makes it easier for skilled AI professionals to secure work permits and establish themselves in the Canadian job market.

Data Science

Canada's data-driven economy has created a massive demand for data science professionals who can collect, analyze, and interpret large volumes of data to drive business decisions and technological innovation. Data science involves the use of statistical methods, machine learning algorithms, and data visualization techniques to extract insights from complex datasets. Canadian businesses across industries; finance, healthcare, retail, manufacturing, and technology, are investing heavily in data-driven strategies to gain a competitive edge. Data science professionals are highly valued in Canada due to the complexity of the work and the impact it has on business outcomes. Data scientists with expertise in programming languages such as Python, R, and SQL, as well as experience with machine learning frameworks like TensorFlow and PyTorch, are particularly in demand. Entry-level data scientists in Canada can expect to earn between CAD $70,000 and $100,000 per year. Experienced data scientists with specialized skills in artificial intelligence, natural language processing, and big data management can command salaries exceeding CAD $150,000, with additional bonuses based on performance and project success.

Data Analytics

Canada's business and government sectors rely heavily on data analytics to make informed decisions and improve performance. Marketing firms use data analytics to track consumer behavior and optimize advertising campaigns. Financial institutions use data analytics to identify investment opportunities and manage portfolio risk. Government agencies use data analytics to improve public services and allocate resources more effectively. Data analysts with strong skills in data visualization, statistical analysis, and business intelligence tools such as Tableau and Power BI are in high demand. Salaries for data analysts in Canada range from CAD $60,000 to $90,000 per year, with senior analysts and business intelligence managers earning over CAD $120,000 annually.

Cybersecurity

Canada's financial sector, healthcare system, and public infrastructure are prime targets for cybercriminals, creating an urgent need for skilled cybersecurity professionals.Cybersecurity professionals in Canada are responsible for securing networks, detecting vulnerabilities, and implementing protective measures against cyber threats. Roles such as security analysts, penetration testers, and incident response specialists are in high demand, with salaries ranging from CAD $80,000 to $150,000 per year. Senior-level positions, such as Chief Information Security Officers (CISOs), can earn salaries exceeding CAD $250,000.

The Canadian government has introduced national cybersecurity strategies and funding programs to strengthen the country's digital defenses. Professionals with certifications such as Certified Information Systems Security Professional (CISSP) and Certified Ethical Hacker (CEH) are highly valued by Canadian employers.

High-Earning Potential in Medical &Legal Fields

Among the most lucrative and stable career paths in canada are the medical and legal fields. These sectors are not only high-paying but also offer strong job security, career progression, and professional recognition. For immigrants and international students seeking to establish themselves in Canada, careers in healthcare and law represent some of the most rewarding opportunities available. The demand for skilled professionals in healthcare and legal services is driven by several key factors, including demographic changes, labor shortages, and the increasing complexity of regulatory and legal frameworks. Canada's aging population has created a growing need for healthcare services, medical innovation, and patient care, while the rise in international trade, corporate expansion, and immigration has increased the demand for legal expertise in business law, immigration law, and family law.

The Canadian government has recognized the strategic importance of attracting professionals in these fields. Targeted immigration programs, such as the Express Entry system and the Provincial Nominee Program (PNP), provide pathways for healthcare professionals and legal experts to secure permanent residency. Canada's healthcare and legal sectors are also heavily regulated, ensuring that professionals who meet the licensing and certification requirements are well-compensated and respected in their respective fields.

Healthcare Professionals

Canada's healthcare sector is experiencing an acute shortage of skilled professionals, driven by an aging population, increased demand for specialized medical services, and the retirement of older healthcare workers. The Canadian government's commitment to providing universal healthcare has created a complex but well-funded healthcare system where medical professionals are highly valued and generously compensated. Doctors, nurses, medical specialists, and healthcare administrators are among the highest-paid professionals in Canada's healthcare system. Family physicians, specialists, and surgeons can earn between CAD $150,000 and $400,000 per year, depending on their level of experience, specialty, and geographic location. In high-demand areas such as rural and northern communities, salaries and incentives for healthcare professionals can be even higher, reflecting the critical need for medical services in underserved regions.

Canada's healthcare system operates on a publicly funded model, where medical services are covered by provincial and territorial health insurance plans. This system ensures that healthcare professionals receive stable and predictable compensation while maintaining a high standard of patient care. However, the shortage of healthcare professionals has placed pressure on the system, leading to longer wait times, reduced access to specialized services, and increased demand for medical innovation.

Legal Professionals

Canada's legal sector is one of the most stable and lucrative fields for skilled professionals. The country's complex legal framework, combined with growing demand for corporate, immigration, and family law services, has created a robust job market for lawyers, legal advisors, and legal consultants. Legal professionals in Canada are highly respected and well-compensated, with opportunities to work in private practice, corporate legal departments, government agencies, and international law firms. Immigration law has become one of the fastest-growing fields within Canada's legal sector. Canada's open immigration policies and increasing volume of immigration applications have created strong demand for immigration lawyers and consultants. Immigration lawyers assist clients with visa applications, residency permits, work permits, and citizenship issues. Successful immigration lawyers can earn between CAD $100,000 and $200,000 annually, with additional compensation for handling complex cases and representing high-net-worth clients.

Legal professionals in Canada are required to complete a law degree (JD or LLB) and pass the bar examination in their respective province or territory. The Law Society of Canada regulates the licensing process, ensuring that legal professionals meet the highest standards of ethics and competence. Foreign-trained lawyers can apply for licensing through the National Committee on Accreditation (NCA), which assesses educational credentials and provides guidance on additional training requirements.

Chapter - 6

Unlocking Business Potential: Exploring Opportunities in Canada

Canada consistently ranks among the top countries for business due to its supportive regulatory framework, competitive tax rates, and government incentives designed to encourage entrepreneurship and innovation. The Canadian business landscape offers a wide range of opportunities across various industries, from the food and beverage industry to Franchising Opportunities.

Food and Beverage Industry: A Thriving Market

Canada's food and beverage industry has witnessed remarkable growth over the past decade, driven by changing consumer preferences, increased disposable income, and a greater emphasis on convenience and health. The industry's resilience during economic downturns and its ability to adapt to changing market conditions make it one of the most stable and attractive sectors for business investment.

The multicultural nature of Canada's population plays a significant role in shaping the food and beverage market. Immigrants account for nearly 22% of Canada's population, bringing with them a rich variety of culinary traditions and dietary preferences. This diversity has created a demand for authentic ethnic cuisine, specialty grocery items, and culturally inspired food products. Restaurants, grocery stores, and food outlets that cater to these diverse tastes have flourished in major urban centers such as Toronto, Vancouver, and Montreal. Canada's supportive business environment and government incentives make it easier for entrepreneurs to enter the food and beverage market. The Canadian government offers funding programs, tax credits, and business grants to support small businesses and encourage innovation in the food industry.

Programs such as the Canada Small Business Financing Program and the Agri-Food Immigration Pilot provide financial assistance and streamlined immigration options for business owners and workers in the food and beverage sector.

Restaurants

Opening a restaurant in Canada is one of the most popular and profitable business ventures in the food and beverage industry. Canada's culinary diversity, combined with its population's growing interest in global cuisine, has created a strong market for new and innovative dining experiences. Restaurants that offer authentic ethnic cuisine, fusion dishes, and locally inspired menus have gained a loyal customer base and attracted positive media attention. The success of ethnic restaurants in Canada reflects the country's multicultural identity. Toronto, often referred to as the most multicultural city in the world, is home to a wide variety of restaurants specializing in Indian, Chinese, Middle Eastern, Italian, Japanese, and Mexican cuisine. Vancouver's proximity to the Pacific Ocean has made it a hotspot for seafood and Asian fusion restaurants, while Montreal's rich French heritage has created a thriving market for French bistros, patisseries, and fine dining establishments.

Technology has played a major role in transforming the restaurant business model. Online ordering, delivery apps, and contactless payment systems have become standard features in the industry. Restaurants that offer delivery through platforms like Uber Eats, DoorDash, and SkipTheDishes have expanded their customer reach and increased sales. Virtual kitchens, where restaurants operate solely through delivery and takeout without a physical dining space, have also gained traction in urban areas. Entrepreneurs entering the restaurant industry in Canada benefit from a range of support services, including commercial kitchen rentals, food incubators, and government-backed training programs. The Restaurant Canada Association provides industry insights, networking opportunities, and advocacy for restaurant owners, helping them navigate regulatory requirements and market trends.

Grocery Stores

Canada's grocery sector has evolved significantly over the past decade, reflecting changes in consumer preferences and shopping behavior. Traditional supermarkets have faced increasing competition from specialty grocery stores, organic markets, and ethnic food retailers. Consumers are seeking high-quality, locally sourced, and culturally diverse food options, creating opportunities for entrepreneurs to establish niche grocery businesses. Specialty grocery stores that focus on organic produce, gluten-free products, and plant-based foods have experienced steady growth in Canada. Health-conscious consumers are willing to pay a premium for products that meet their dietary preferences and ethical standards. Grocery stores that partner with local farmers and food producers to offer farm-to-table options have gained a competitive edge in attracting loyal customers.

Ethnic grocery stores have also flourished in Canada's multicultural cities. In neighborhoods with large immigrant populations, grocery stores specializing in Asian, Middle Eastern, South Asian, and Latin American products have become important community hubs. These stores offer hard-to-find ingredients, imported goods, and culturally specific food products that cater to the tastes and cooking traditions of local residents. Online grocery shopping has emerged as a major trend in Canada's food retail market. Supermarkets and independent grocery stores have introduced online ordering, curbside pickup, and home delivery services to meet the demand for convenience. The expansion of e-commerce in the grocery sector has created new opportunities for entrepreneurs to establish online specialty food stores and direct-to-consumer delivery platforms.

Food Franchises and Takeaway Counters

Franchising has become one of the most popular entry points for entrepreneurs seeking to establish a business in Canada's food and beverage industry. Well-known franchises such as Tim Hortons, Subway, McDonald's, and Pizza Pizza offer proven business models, brand recognition, and operational support to franchise owners. Food franchisees benefit from established customer bases, marketing support, and standardized operating procedures, reducing the risk associated with starting a business from scratch. Fast-food franchises, coffee chains, and quick-service restaurants have become highly profitable due to their ability to generate consistent sales and adapt to changing consumer preferences. Takeaway counters and food stalls in malls, airports, and food courts offer another scalable business model. These outlets have lower overhead costs than traditional restaurants and benefit from high foot traffic in busy commercial areas. Entrepreneurs who operate takeaway counters can focus on offering quick, affordable, and high-quality food options tailored to the local market.

Entrepreneurs who understand the local market, leverage technological advancements, and deliver high-quality food products will find long-term success in Canada's thriving food and beverage sector. For immigrants and international business owners, the food industry represents a pathway to economic independence, professional success, and long-term financial security.

Retail and Service-Based Businesses

Canada's entrepreneurial landscape is thriving, with retail and service-based businesses playing a significant role in the country's economy. These businesses cater to the everyday needs of consumers, providing essential goods and services while creating employment opportunities and driving economic growth. The retail sector in Canada contributes billions of dollars to the economy annually, while the service industry continues to expand due to changing consumer lifestyles, increased disposable income, and a growing demand for convenience.

For immigrants and aspiring entrepreneurs, retail and service-based businesses offer a promising pathway to financial independence and long-term business success. Unlike industries that require extensive technical expertise or large-scale investment, retail and service-based businesses provide accessible opportunities for entrepreneurs with diverse backgrounds and skill sets. Whether it's opening a convenience store, launching a health and fitness business, or tapping into the lucrative pet services market, these business models allow individuals to address specific consumer needs and build sustainable enterprises.

Convenience Stores and Pharmacy

Convenience stores and pharmacies are some of the most resilient businesses in Canada, providing consumers with quick access to essential products such as groceries, snacks, beverages, personal care items, and over-the-counter medications. These businesses thrive in urban and suburban areas where customers prioritize convenience and accessibility. Convenience stores, also known as corner stores or variety stores, are a staple of Canadian communities. They serve as quick-stop locations for busy consumers who need to purchase small quantities of everyday items without making a trip to a large supermarket. These stores are particularly successful in high-traffic areas such as residential neighborhoods, near public transit stations, and in proximity to schools and workplaces.

The key to running a successful convenience store in Canada lies in offering a well-curated selection of products that meet consumer demand. In addition to traditional grocery items, many convenience stores have expanded their offerings to include fresh produce, pre-packaged meals, lottery tickets, mobile phone accessories, and even locally made products. Entrepreneurs who strategically stock their stores with high-demand items and offer competitive pricing can build a loyal customer base and generate steady revenue. Entrepreneurs looking to establish a pharmacy must navigate regulatory requirements, including obtaining a pharmacy license and working with licensed pharmacists to dispense medications.

Health and Fitness

The health and fitness industry in Canada has experienced significant growth in recent years, driven by increased consumer awareness of the importance of physical well-being, preventive healthcare, and overall wellness. Canadians are actively seeking ways to stay fit, improve their mental health, and adopt healthier lifestyles, creating a lucrative market for entrepreneurs in the health and fitness space.

Gyms and fitness centers have become increasingly popular, with many Canadians investing in memberships to maintain an active lifestyle. The demand for specialized fitness programs, including yoga, pilates, high-intensity interval training (HIIT), and personal training services, has surged as consumers seek more tailored fitness solutions. Entrepreneurs looking to enter the fitness industry can establish boutique fitness studios, personal training services, or franchise well-known gym brands such as GoodLife Fitness and F45 Training. The rise of digital fitness platforms has also created new business opportunities in the industry. Online fitness coaching, virtual workout programs, and mobile fitness apps allow entrepreneurs to reach a broader audience without the overhead costs of operating a physical gym. Trainers and wellness coaches who leverage social media, streaming platforms, and subscription-based workout plans can build profitable businesses with global reach.

Nutrition and wellness services complement the fitness industry and provide additional revenue streams for entrepreneurs. Health-conscious consumers are seeking professional guidance on weight management, meal planning, and dietary supplements. Businesses that offer personalized nutrition coaching, meal prep services, and specialty health food products are thriving in Canada's wellness-focused market. Corporate wellness programs represent another emerging trend in Canada's health and fitness industry. Companies are investing in employee wellness initiatives to improve workplace productivity, reduce healthcare costs, and promote a positive work environment. Entrepreneurs who offer corporate wellness consulting, workplace fitness programs, and mental health workshops can secure contracts with businesses looking to prioritize employee well-being.

Pet Services and Products:

The pet industry in Canada is booming, driven by the country's growing number of pet owners who view their pets as valued family members. Canadians are spending more on pet care than ever before, investing in high-quality pet products, premium pet food, grooming services, and specialized veterinary care. Entrepreneurs looking to enter the pet services and products market can capitalize on this growing demand and build successful businesses that cater to pet owner's needs. Pet grooming services are in high demand, with many pet owners seeking professional grooming to maintain their pet's hygiene and appearance. Grooming salons offer services such as bathing, fur trimming, nail clipping, and specialty treatments for pets with specific grooming needs. Mobile pet grooming services have gained popularity as well, providing pet owners with the convenience of at-home grooming for their pets.

The rise of pet-friendly workplaces and pet-inclusive lifestyles has also contributed to the growth of pet daycare and boarding services. Busy professionals and frequent travelers rely on pet daycare facilities to provide safe and comfortable environments for their pets while they are away. Luxury pet hotels and specialized boarding services have emerged to cater to pet owners who want premium care for their animals, including personalized playtime, specialized diets, and veterinary supervision. Pet health and wellness products have become a major industry trend in Canada. Consumers are increasingly interested in organic pet food, natural supplements, and sustainable pet care products. Entrepreneurs who launch eco-friendly pet product lines, subscription-based pet food delivery services, or specialty pet boutiques can tap into this expanding market and attract health-conscious pet owners.

Pet training and behavioral consulting services have also gained traction in Canada. As more Canadians adopt pets, the need for professional training programs has increased. Dog trainers, animal behaviorists, and pet obedience schools provide valuable services that help pet owners develop well-behaved and socialized pets. The pet industry's continued growth presents a unique opportunity for entrepreneurs who are passionate about animals and customer service. Businesses that offer high-quality pet services, innovative pet products, and exceptional customer experiences can build lasting brands in Canada's thriving pet market.

E-Commerce and Online Ventures:

The rise of digital technology has transformed the global business landscape, creating new opportunities for entrepreneurs to build successful online ventures. Canada has emerged as one of the fastest-growing e-commerce markets, fueled by a tech-savvy population, high internet penetration, and a strong digital economy. With consumers increasingly turning to online platforms for shopping, entertainment, and services, entrepreneurs can tap into this ever-growing market and establish profitable e-commerce and digital businesses. Canada's supportive business environment, secure digital infrastructure, and government initiatives to promote innovation have made it an ideal location for launching and scaling online ventures. The demand for e-commerce solutions, digital marketing services, and online consulting continues to grow as businesses seek to expand their online presence and reach a global audience. Entrepreneurs who understand digital consumer behavior, leverage data-driven strategies, and stay ahead of technological trends can build successful online enterprises that generate long-term revenue.

Online Retail:

E-commerce has revolutionized the way Canadians shop, with online retail sales reaching record levels in recent years. The convenience, variety, and accessibility of online shopping have led to a shift in consumer behavior, with more people preferring to purchase goods and services through digital platforms rather than traditional brick-and-mortar stores. Entrepreneurs who enter the online retail market can tap into this growing trend and build thriving businesses that cater to changing consumer demands. The COVID-19 pandemic accelerated the adoption of e-commerce in Canada, with businesses of all sizes investing in digital transformation to meet customer needs. Consumers are now more comfortable than ever with online shopping, leading to sustained growth in the industry. The rise of mobile commerce (m-commerce) has further fueled this expansion, as more Canadians use smartphones and tablets to make purchases.

Starting an online retail business in Canada requires an understanding of market trends, consumer preferences, and digital sales channels. Entrepreneurs can choose from various business models, including dropshipping, print-on-demand, private labeling, and direct-to-consumer (DTC) retail. Each model offers unique advantages, allowing business owners to tailor their approach based on investment levels, industry expertise, and target audiences. Dropshipping is one of the most popular e-commerce business models, particularly for entrepreneurs who want to start an online store without managing inventory. With dropshipping, business owners partner with third-party suppliers who handle product fulfillment and shipping. This model minimizes upfront costs and operational complexities, making it an attractive option for new e-commerce entrepreneurs. Platforms such as Shopify, WooCommerce, and BigCommerce provide user-friendly tools to set up and manage dropshipping businesses, enabling entrepreneurs to focus on marketing and customer acquisition.

Print-on-demand is another viable e-commerce business model that allows entrepreneurs to sell custom-designed products such as clothing, accessories, and home decor without holding inventory. Print-on-demand platforms like Printful and Teespring handle production and shipping, allowing business owners to create unique products and sell them globally. This model is particularly popular among artists, designers, and content creators looking to monetize their brand through customized merchandise. Private labeling and direct-to-consumer (DTC) e-commerce involve sourcing or manufacturing products under a unique brand name and selling them directly to consumers. This model provides greater control over branding, pricing, and customer experience. Entrepreneurs who develop high-quality products and build strong brand identities can differentiate themselves in competitive markets and establish long-term customer loyalty.

The key to success in online retail lies in strategic marketing, user experience optimization, and effective supply chain management. Digital marketing tools such as search engine optimization (SEO), social media advertising, and influencer partnerships play a crucial role in driving traffic and conversions for online stores. Entrepreneurs who invest in high-quality product photography, compelling product descriptions, and seamless checkout processes can enhance the online shopping experience and increase customer retention. Canada's e-commerce ecosystem also benefits from reliable logistics and shipping infrastructure. Major carriers such as Canada Post, FedEx, and UPS offer efficient delivery services that support the growth of online retail businesses. Entrepreneurs can leverage fulfillment services such as Amazon FBA (Fulfillment by Amazon) to streamline order processing and reach a wider audience.

Sustainability has become a significant trend in e-commerce, with consumers increasingly seeking eco-friendly products and ethical business practices. Online retailers who prioritize sustainable sourcing, biodegradable packaging, and transparent supply chains can attract environmentally conscious consumers and differentiate themselves in the market.

Digital Marketing and Consulting:

As more businesses shift their focus to online platforms, the demand for digital marketing and consulting services has surged. Companies of all sizes are investing in digital strategies to enhance their online presence, attract customers, and drive sales. Entrepreneurs with expertise in digital marketing, social media management, and business consulting can capitalize on this growing demand and build profitable service-based businesses. SEO is one of the most critical components of digital marketing, as it helps businesses improve their rankings on search engines such as Google and Bing. Entrepreneurs who specialize in SEO optimization can offer services such as keyword research, website audits, and content strategy development to help businesses increase organic traffic and online visibility. With competition in the digital space growing, companies are willing to invest in professional SEO services to gain a competitive edge.

Content marketing and copywriting services are also valuable in the digital landscape. Businesses need high-quality content to educate their audiences, improve brand credibility, and drive traffic to their websites. Entrepreneurs with strong writing skills can provide blog writing, video script development, and website content creation services to businesses looking to enhance their digital marketing efforts.

The e-commerce has also created demand for business consultants who can guide entrepreneurs in scaling their online ventures. E-commerce consultants provide expertise in website optimization, conversion rate improvement, customer retention strategies, and financial planning. Entrepreneurs who have successfully built online businesses can leverage their experience to offer consulting services to aspiring e-commerce business owners. Canada's business-friendly policies and access to global markets make it an ideal location for launching digital marketing and consulting businesses. Entrepreneurs in these fields can operate remotely, scale their businesses through online networking, and work with clients worldwide. The ability to offer digital services without the need for physical storefronts or inventory makes digital marketing and consulting highly profitable and scalable.

Service-Based Businesses for Community Needs

Canada is home to diverse and vibrant communities that continuously seek high-quality, reliable services to support their daily lives. As the country experiences economic growth, urban expansion, and population increases, the demand for essential service-based businesses continues to rise. Entrepreneurs looking to establish a business in Canada can find immense success by offering valuable services that cater to community needs. Whether it is providing professional cleaning services or home renovation and repair solutions, these businesses not only generate strong revenue but also create meaningful employment opportunities and contribute to the well-being of local communities. Service-based businesses offer several advantages for entrepreneurs, including lower startup costs compared to product-based ventures, the ability to operate with minimal inventory, and the potential for recurring customers. Many of these businesses require skill-based expertise rather than significant capital investment, making them an attractive option for newcomers, international business owners, and skilled tradespeople.

As Canada's real estate market continues to expand and more homeowners invest in property maintenance and improvement, service-based industries that cater to household needs are experiencing significant growth. The demand for reliable, professional, and high-quality services in cleaning, home renovation, and repair has made these sectors highly lucrative for entrepreneurs. By identifying gaps in the market, understanding customer preferences, and prioritizing service excellence, business owners can establish themselves as trusted providers in their respective industries.

Cleaning Services

The cleaning services industry in Canada has experienced remarkable growth over the years, driven by an increasing number of dual-income households, busy professionals, and businesses seeking outsourced cleaning solutions. The demand for cleaning services spans across residential, commercial, and industrial sectors, making it a versatile and recession-resistant business. As people place greater emphasis on cleanliness and hygiene, particularly in the wake of global health concerns, cleaning services have become an essential part of everyday life.

Starting a cleaning service business in Canada requires minimal initial investment compared to other service-based businesses. Entrepreneurs can start small with a few essential supplies and gradually expand as they acquire more clients. Whether operating as an independent contractor or establishing a larger cleaning company, the potential for growth is significant. Many cleaning businesses operate on a recurring basis, offering weekly, biweekly, or monthly services, which ensures a steady stream of income and long-term customer retention.

Commercial cleaning services also offer a lucrative business opportunity. Offices, retail spaces, schools, medical facilities, and restaurants require routine cleaning and maintenance to ensure a hygienic and professional environment. Many businesses outsource their cleaning needs to third-party service providers, creating a continuous demand for reliable cleaning companies. Entrepreneurs who establish contracts with businesses, government institutions, and corporate offices can generate significant revenue and scale their operations quickly. Specialized cleaning services, such as eco-friendly cleaning, carpet and upholstery cleaning, and industrial deep cleaning, provide additional avenues for business growth. As more Canadians seek environmentally friendly solutions, green cleaning services that use non-toxic and biodegradable products have gained popularity. Offering sustainable cleaning solutions can differentiate a business from competitors and attract environmentally conscious consumers. The success of a cleaning business in Canada relies heavily on reputation, customer satisfaction, and efficient service delivery. Entrepreneurs who focus on hiring well-trained staff, using high-quality cleaning products, and providing excellent customer service can establish themselves as leaders in the industry. Additionally, leveraging digital marketing, customer referrals, and online booking platforms can help cleaning businesses reach a wider audience and secure long-term contracts.

The cleaning services industry offers a resilient and scalable business model that can be adapted to various market needs. Entrepreneurs who enter this sector with a strategic approach, strong customer focus, and high service standards can achieve long-term profitability and business success in Canada's growing service economy.

Home Renovation and Repair Services

Canada's housing market continues to be one of the most active in the world, with homeowners investing heavily in renovations, repairs, and property upgrades. The demand for home renovation and repair services has skyrocketed as homeowners seek to enhance their living spaces, increase property value, and address maintenance issues. Entrepreneurs who enter this industry can capitalize on the growing trend of home improvement, providing essential services that cater to property owners, real estate investors, and commercial property managers.

Home renovation and repair services encompass a wide range of specialized trades, including carpentry, plumbing, electrical work, roofing, flooring, and interior design. Skilled professionals who offer these services are in high demand, as homeowners often require expert assistance for home improvement projects that go beyond simple do-it-yourself (DIY) fixes. The industry presents an excellent opportunity for skilled workers, general contractors, and entrepreneurs looking to establish a reputable business in Canada's booming housing sector..

The Canadian government has also introduced various incentives and rebate programs for homeowners who undertake eco-friendly home improvements. Entrepreneurs who specialize in green renovations, such as energy-efficient window installations, solar panel installations, and smart home technology integration, can tap into a rapidly expanding market. Consumers are more willing to invest in renovations that reduce their energy bills, improve sustainability, and increase the long-term value of their properties.

Emergency repair services are another high-demand sector within the home improvement industry. Homeowners frequently require urgent repairs for plumbing leaks, electrical failures, roof damage, and heating system malfunctions. Businesses that offer 24/7 emergency repair services can command premium rates while building a reputation for reliability and prompt service.

Property management companies and real estate investors represent an additional market for renovation and repair businesses. Rental properties require regular maintenance and occasional upgrades to remain competitive in the rental market. Entrepreneurs who establish contracts with property management firms to handle routine repairs, tenant move-out renovations, and apartment upgrades can create a steady stream of business.

The home renovation and repair industry requires compliance with building codes, safety regulations, and licensing requirements. Entrepreneurs must ensure they have the proper certifications and permits to operate legally and maintain credibility with clients. Hiring skilled tradespeople, using high-quality materials, and adhering to industry best practices are crucial for long-term success in this field.

Franchising Opportunities

Canada's business landscape is filled with opportunities for entrepreneurs seeking financial success, stability, and long-term growth. While starting an independent business can be rewarding, it comes with significant risks, including brand building, marketing challenges, and operational complexities. Franchising presents a unique solution for aspiring business owners who want to enter the market with a pre-established business model, access to brand recognition, and ongoing support from a franchisor. The franchising model has proven to be highly successful in Canada, with thousands of franchise businesses operating across various industries, including food and beverage, fitness, retail, and service-based enterprises. Franchises provide entrepreneurs with a structured roadmap to success, offering standardized products, training programs, and operational support. For immigrants and international entrepreneurs, franchising is an attractive option as it minimizes the uncertainties associated with starting a business from scratch and provides a clear pathway to financial independence.

Canada's franchise industry continues to expand, driven by consumer demand for established brands, trusted service providers, and consistent customer experiences. With strong support from franchise associations, financial institutions, and government programs, entrepreneurs can access the necessary resources to successfully invest in a franchise business. Understanding the different types of franchises available and choosing the right industry is essential for long-term success.

Types of Franchises to Consider

Canada's franchising market is diverse, with opportunities available across multiple industries. Entrepreneurs should consider their interests, skills, and financial resources when selecting a franchise to invest in. Some of the most popular and profitable franchise categories include food and beverage, fitness, and retail/service franchises.

Food and Beverage: International Chains, Casual Dining, and Quick-Service Food

The food and beverage industry is one of the most lucrative and stable sectors for franchising in Canada. With a strong demand for dining options, coffee shops, and quick-service restaurants, food franchises offer excellent revenue potential and long-term growth opportunities. The success of food franchises is driven by brand recognition, customer loyalty, and consistent product offerings. Quick-service restaurants (QSRs) are among the most popular food franchises. Well-known brands such as McDonald's, Tim Hortons, Subway, and Pizza Pizza dominate the Canadian market, providing franchisees with a ready-made customer base and established operational procedures. These franchises benefit from high foot traffic, strong marketing support, and streamlined supply chain management.

Casual dining restaurants and family-friendly eateries also present strong franchising opportunities. Brands such as Boston Pizza, Kelseys, and The Keg have built loyal customer bases and continue to expand across Canada. Casual dining franchises typically require a larger investment than QSRs, but they offer higher profit margins and opportunities for long-term business growth.

Coffee shops and specialty beverage franchises have also seen tremendous success in Canada. With a strong coffee culture and a growing demand for specialty drinks, franchises such as Starbucks, Second Cup, and Booster Juice have become highly profitable ventures. Entrepreneurs looking to enter the beverage industry can benefit from Canada's high consumer demand for premium coffee, smoothies, and wellness-focused drinks.

For entrepreneurs interested in niche markets, specialty food franchises offer unique opportunities. Health-conscious consumers are seeking organic, plant-based, and gluten-free dining options, creating demand for franchises that focus on sustainable and nutritious food. Brands such as Freshii and Pita Pit have capitalized on this trend, offering healthy alternatives to traditional fast food.

Fitness: Gym Franchises and Wellness-Focused Businesses

The health and wellness industry in Canada has seen remarkable growth, with consumers increasingly prioritizing fitness, mental well-being, and healthy lifestyles. Gym franchises and wellness-focused businesses offer excellent opportunities for entrepreneurs looking to invest in a business that promotes health and personal development. Gym franchises, such as GoodLife Fitness, Anytime Fitness, and F45 Training, have become highly successful in Canada, offering flexible workout solutions for different customer demographics. With a growing emphasis on fitness and preventative health, gym memberships have increased, leading to a steady revenue stream for franchise owners. Wellness-focused businesses, including massage therapy, physiotherapy, and holistic health centers, present additional franchising opportunities. Consumers are seeking alternative health solutions to manage stress, improve mobility, and enhance overall well-being. Franchises such as Massage Addict and The Stretch Lab offer specialized wellness services that cater to this growing market.

Retail and Service Franchises: Mobile Services, Cleaning, Tutoring, and Retail Chains

Retail and service-based franchises are among the most accessible and scalable business opportunities in Canada. Entrepreneurs who prefer a business model with lower overhead costs and flexible operations can explore mobile services, cleaning franchises, tutoring centers, and retail chains. Mobile service franchises, such as automotive detailing, locksmith services, and home maintenance, provide convenience to customers by offering services at their doorstep. These franchises typically require lower startup costs and can be operated from a home office, making them ideal for first-time business owners.

Cleaning franchises, including residential and commercial cleaning services, offer recession-proof business opportunities. With a growing demand for professional cleaning solutions, brands such as Molly Maid and JAN-PRO have established themselves as industry leaders. Cleaning franchises benefit from repeat business, strong customer loyalty, and low operational costs.

Tutoring and education franchises have become increasingly popular as parents seek additional academic support for their children. Brands such as Sylvan Learning and Kumon provide structured learning programs that help students improve their academic performance. Entrepreneurs who invest in tutoring franchises can contribute to their communities while generating consistent revenue.

Retail chain franchises, including clothing stores, convenience stores, and specialty shops, continue to thrive in Canada. Established brands such as 7-Eleven, The UPS Store, and Dollarama offer franchisees the advantage of a well-known brand name and proven business strategies.

Chapter - 7

The Canada Start-Up Visa: The Pathway to Permanent Residency for Entrepreneurs

Canada has established itself as one of the most welcoming countries for entrepreneurs and business owners seeking to expand their ventures internationally. With its stable economy, strong government support for innovation, and business-friendly policies, Canada offers an ideal environment for start-ups and enterprises to thrive. Recognizing the value that foreign entrepreneurs bring to the economy, the Canadian government introduced the Start-Up Visa (SUV) Program, a unique immigration pathway that allows innovative business owners to obtain permanent residency while launching their businesses in Canada. The Start-Up Visa is particularly attractive to international entrepreneurs who want to establish a business in a country known for its strong economy, diverse consumer base, and access to global markets. Unlike many other business immigration programs, which require substantial upfront investment or a history of business success, the Start-Up Visa focuses on the potential of innovative business ideas. Entrepreneurs with scalable business concepts, particularly in technology, digital solutions, artificial intelligence, healthcare, and green energy, stand a strong chance of securing permanent residency through this program.

For students, entrepreneurs, and immigrants planning to move to Canada, the Start-Up Visa presents a valuable opportunity not just to gain residency but also to integrate into Canada's dynamic business ecosystem. This program is designed to help high-potential start-ups succeed by connecting them with designated venture capital funds, angel investors, and business incubators. By securing support from these designated organizations, entrepreneurs can access funding, mentorship, and resources needed to build a sustainable business in Canada.

Why the Start-Up Visa is the Best Immigration Program

For aspiring entrepreneurs seeking permanent residency in Canada, the Start-Up Visa (SUV) Program stands out as one of the most attractive immigration pathways. Unlike traditional immigration programs that focus on education credentials, work experience, or high personal investment, the Start-Up Visa is uniquely designed to attract innovative business minds from around the world. Canada recognizes that economic growth and job creation depend on entrepreneurship, and through this program, the country welcomes individuals with scalable business ideas who can contribute to the economy while securing their long-term future in Canada. The Start-Up Visa offers a streamlined and entrepreneur-friendly pathway to permanent residency, making it one of the most sought-after immigration programs. The program's flexibility, inclusivity, and low financial burden make it an excellent choice for entrepreneurs who may not qualify for other Canadian immigration programs due to stringent eligibility criteria. Whether one is a seasoned business professional or a young entrepreneur with a fresh, innovative idea, the Start-Up Visa provides a fair, accessible, and highly rewarding path to Canadian residency and business success.

What sets the Start-Up Visa apart from other immigration programs is that it does not impose education requirements, age restrictions, or a minimum investment threshold. Additionally, its language proficiency requirement is significantly lower compared to other pathways, making it an ideal option for entrepreneurs from diverse backgrounds who may not have perfect English or French skills but possess strong business acumen.

This chapter explores the specific advantages of the Start-Up Visa Program, detailing why it is one of the best immigration programs available for entrepreneurs and how applicants can maximize this opportunity.

No Educational Requirements

One of the most significant barriers for many skilled professionals and entrepreneurs when applying for permanent residency in Canada is the education requirement. Many traditional immigration pathways, such as the Express Entry system, require applicants to hold at least a bachelor's degree to gain a competitive Comprehensive Ranking System (CRS) score.

The Start-Up Visa, however, does not impose any minimum educational requirement. This is a game-changer for entrepreneurs who may not have formal higher education but have the practical skills, business acumen, and experience to launch and run a successful business. Canada understands that some of the world's greatest entrepreneurs, including Steve Jobs, Bill Gates, and Mark Zuckerberg, never completed university degrees. Instead, their success was built on vision, execution, and persistence rather than formal education. The absence of an educational requirement in the Start-Up Visa program makes it accessible to self-made entrepreneurs, industry experts, and business visionaries who have learned through real-world experience rather than traditional classroom education. Many entrepreneurs in technology, digital innovation, and the service industry have built highly successful companies despite lacking formal academic qualifications. The Canadian government acknowledges this reality and offers a path to permanent residency for entrepreneurs based on business potential rather than degrees. For entrepreneurs who may have dropped out of university to start a business, pursued alternative education paths, or gained expertise through work experience, the Start-Up Visa provides a once-in-a-lifetime opportunity to secure Canadian residency without academic restrictions.

No Age Criteria

Age is often a deciding factor in many immigration programs worldwide, with younger applicants typically favored over older professionals. Programs like Express Entry and Provincial Nominee Programs (PNPs) assign more points to applicants between 20 and 35 years old, meaning older applicants often struggle to meet the required CRS cut-off. However, the Start-Up Visa does not have any age limit or restrictions, making it one of the most inclusive immigration programs in Canada. Entrepreneurs of any age, whether they are in their 20s, mid-career professionals, or even experienced business owners in their 50s or 60s, can apply without worrying about age-related point reductions.

The flexibility in age criteria ensures that Canada attracts entrepreneurs with varied experiences, backgrounds, and industry expertise. Some of the world's most successful businesses were founded by individuals in their 40s, 50s, and beyond. Colonel Sanders, the founder of KFC, started his business in his 60s. Ray Kroc, who turned McDonald's into a global empire, was in his 50s when he expanded the franchise. For many experienced business professionals, moving to Canada through traditional immigration programs can be difficult due to age restrictions. Even if they have years of industry experience, a strong business network, and the ability to contribute significantly to the economy, their applications may receive fewer points in age-based systems.

The Start-Up Visa ensures that no talented entrepreneur is excluded based on age. Whether an applicant is a young innovator with a cutting-edge technology start-up or an experienced businessperson looking to expand their company in Canada, the program provides an equal opportunity for all.

No Minimum Investment Requirement

Most business immigration programs worldwide require entrepreneurs to make substantial personal investments to qualify. For example, Canada's Provincial Nominee Entrepreneur Programs (PNP-Entrepreneur Streams) often require applicants to invest between CAD $150,000 and CAD $600,000 into a business before they can apply for permanent residency. The Start-Up Visa, however, does not require any minimum investment from the applicant. Instead, entrepreneurs only need to secure support from a designated organization—which can be a venture capital firm, angel investor group, or business incubator. These designated organizations evaluate the business idea and provide funding, mentorship, and networking opportunities to help entrepreneurs establish their businesses in Canada.

By removing the personal investment requirement, the Start-Up Visa makes immigration accessible to a wider range of entrepreneurs who may have brilliant business ideas but limited capital. Many tech start-ups and digital businesses do not require large upfront investments; instead, they focus on scalability, innovation, and market disruption. For aspiring business owners who do not have large savings or personal assets but have the ability to attract investment and build a successful company, the Start-Up Visa provides an unmatched opportunity to move to Canada without the burden of personal financial commitments.

Flexible Language Requirements

Many immigration programs in Canada have strict language requirements, often requiring applicants to achieve a high Canadian Language Benchmark (CLB) score in English or French. Programs like Express Entry demand CLB 7 or higher, which can be challenging for non-native speakers. The Start-Up Visa, however, has a more lenient language requirement. Applicants only need to achieve CLB 5 in either English or French, which is significantly lower than what is required for other immigration pathways. This flexible requirement ensures that entrepreneurs with strong business potential are not excluded due to language barriers. While communication is important in business, the Canadian government recognizes that successful entrepreneurs can hire managers, translators, or local employees to assist with language needs. To summarize, you need only IELTS 5554 where 4 is in the reading section while 5 in the rest sections of Listening, Writing and Speaking.

How the Start-Up Visa Works

Canada's Start-Up Visa (SUV) Program is one of the most innovative immigration pathways in the world. Unlike traditional business immigration programs that require applicants to demonstrate substantial personal wealth, financial stability, or prior business success, the Start-Up Visa focuses entirely on innovation, scalability, and the economic impact of a business idea. This approach ensures that entrepreneurs with great ideas—but limited capital—still have a fair chance to establish themselves in Canada and obtain permanent residency. The key requirement of the Start-Up Visa is securing a Letter of Support from a designated Canadian organization, such as a business incubator, angel investor group, or venture capital fund. This designated entity must evaluate the applicant's business proposal and determine whether it has strong potential for growth, innovation, and job creation in Canada. Once the applicant receives this Letter of Support, they can apply for permanent residency and begin building their business in Canada.

This process ensures that only genuinely promising start-ups make their way into the Canadian market, fostering economic growth and technological advancement. Unlike programs that rely on financial assets as a qualifier, the Start-Up Visa prioritizes business potential, entrepreneurship, and contribution to the Canadian economy. For students, international business owners, and immigrants planning to move to Canada, understanding how the Start-Up Visa works is crucial for successfully navigating the application process and maximizing business opportunities. This chapter provides an in-depth exploration of the step-by-step process, requirements, and advantages of this unique immigration program.

Key Requirements for the Start-Up Visa Program

The Start-Up Visa (SUV) Program offers a unique opportunity for entrepreneurs to gain permanent residency in Canada while building innovative businesses. However, applicants must meet specific requirements to qualify. These criteria ensure that only high-potential entrepreneurs with viable business ideas and strong market potential are selected.

Business Idea with Strong Growth Potential

The foundation of a successful Start-Up Visa application is a high-potential business idea that demonstrates innovation, scalability, and economic impact. Canada seeks entrepreneurs who can introduce new technologies, create jobs, and contribute to the country's economic growth. Businesses in technology, clean energy, artificial intelligence, fintech, and healthcare are particularly attractive under this program. The business must be original, competitive, and capable of expanding beyond the local market.

Letter of Support from a Designated Entity

A crucial requirement for the Start-Up Visa is securing a Letter of Support from a designated organization in Canada. This letter serves as proof that the business has been reviewed and approved by an official investment or mentorship entity. The designated entity can be one of the following: An incubator is a business accelerator that provides mentorship, office space, and strategic guidance to help start-ups succeed. Entrepreneurs must be accepted into a Canadian incubator program to qualify for the Start-Up Visa. An angel investor is a private investment group that funds early-stage businesses with high growth potential. To qualify under this category, applicants must secure a minimum investment of CAD $75,000 from a government-designated angel investor group. A venture capitalist is an investment firm that provides large-scale funding to innovative start-ups. Entrepreneurs who receive a minimum investment of CAD $200,000 from a venture capital fund automatically meet the requirement for the Start-Up Visa. Once a Letter of Support is secured from any of these designated entities, the applicant can proceed with their permanent residency application.

Language Proficiency Requirement

Entrepreneurs applying for the Start-Up Visa must demonstrate basic proficiency in English or French. The language requirement is set at Canadian Language Benchmark (CLB) level 5, which is lower than what is required for many other immigration programs. This means that applicants need only a moderate level of fluency to qualify. The most commonly used language test for the Start-Up Visa is the IELTS (International English Language Testing System). The required scores for eligibility are 5 in speaking, 5 in listening, 5 in reading, and 4 in writing. This language benchmark ensures that entrepreneurs can communicate effectively in business environments and engage with customers, investors, and employees in Canada.

Proof of Funds Requirement

While applicants are not required to make a personal financial investment in their business, they must demonstrate sufficient funds to support themselves and their family upon arrival in Canada. This financial proof ensures that entrepreneurs can cover living expenses until their business becomes profitable. The required amount depends on the number of family members accompanying the applicant and is updated annually by Immigration, Refugees, and Citizenship Canada (IRCC). The proof of funds can be shown through bank statements, fixed deposits, or other liquid financial assets. These funds must be readily available and not tied to real estate or business investments. The Start-Up Visa program is designed to attract talented, driven, and innovative entrepreneurs who can contribute to Canada's economy. By meeting the key requirements, a strong business idea, a Letter of Support, language proficiency, and proof of funds, applicants can secure permanent residency and take advantage of Canada's thriving start-up ecosystem.

Securing Capital: (Business Funding through Banks, Incubators, Angel Investors, and Venture Capitalists)

Access to funding is one of the most critical aspects of launching and scaling a business. Entrepreneurs must secure financial backing to cover operational costs, invest in growth opportunities, and ensure long-term sustainability. Canada offers multiple funding avenues, ranging from traditional bank loans and government grants to high-risk, high-reward investments from venture capitalists and angel investors. Understanding these funding options and how to attract investors is essential for business success.

Bank Loans and Government Grants for Entrepreneurs

Banks and financial institutions in Canada provide a variety of loan programs designed specifically for entrepreneurs. These loans offer competitive interest rates and structured repayment plans that allow businesses to manage their finances effectively. Many banks have dedicated small business departments that help start-ups secure funding based on their business plans, creditworthiness, and projected revenue.

Venture Capital and Angel Investors for High-Growth Businesses

For businesses with high growth potential, venture capital firms and angel investors provide an alternative to traditional funding. These investors offer significant financial backing in exchange for equity, allowing businesses to scale quickly. Venture capital firms typically invest in technology-driven, scalable start-ups that demonstrate strong revenue potential. They not only provide funding but also offer strategic mentorship, industry connections, and access to global markets. Angel investors, on the other hand, are individuals or small groups who invest in early-stage businesses. They lock for innovative ideas with strong leadership and the potential for rapid expansion. Unlike venture capitalists, angel investors often take a more personal approach, mentoring entrepreneurs and guiding them through early growth stages.

Crafting Compelling Proposals to Secure Funding and Scale Operations

To attract funding, entrepreneurs must develop a compelling business proposal that clearly outlines their market potential, revenue projections, and competitive advantage. A well-structured pitch should highlight the problem the business solves, the scalability of the solution, and the financial returns investors can expect. Strong financial planning, data-backed projections, and a clear growth strategy increase the likelihood of securing funding. Networking plays a crucial role in the funding process. Entrepreneurs should actively engage with incubators, accelerators, and business mentorship programs to build connections with potential investors. Attending start-up events, pitching competitions, and investor meetups provides direct access to funding sources and increases visibility within the industry.

Securing capital is a crucial step in building a successful business. By exploring multiple funding avenues; whether through banks, government programs, venture capitalists, or angel investors; entrepreneurs can access the financial resources needed to fuel innovation and long-term growth.

What kind of businesses go under Start UP Visa?

Author's Insight: The Start-Up Visa program requires an innovative business concept, often involving technologies such as Artificial Intelligence, Machine Learning, or other novel solutions. However, innovation doesn't always mean tech-heavy ideas; it can also include concepts focused on sustainability, energy efficiency, or green initiatives.

I have personally worked on Start-Up Visa projects across a wide range of industries. Here are a few examples that illustrate the diversity and creativity possible within this program:

- **Dish Designer**: A unique concept in the food industry, allowing customers to personalize their daily tiffins based on dietary needs and preferences. The platform integrates a dietician's guidance with an AI-powered food app. Users enter personal metrics such as height, weight, and age, then select fitness goals, such as weight loss or muscle gain. The app generates meal recommendations accordingly, combining health and convenience.

- **Legal Assist**: A global legal collaboration platform where lawyers across various specialties, criminal, civil, immigration, arbitration, and matrimonial, can connect, consult, and even share profits. It serves both legal professionals and end users, creating a digital marketplace for legal expertise and collaboration.

- **Voyage Nova**: An edtech tourism platform that brings history and science to life. Students can travel to historical locations to deepen their learning or enroll in science-focused tours such as NASA field trips. It's an experiential learning model that bridges education and exploration.

- **Mail Booth**: This innovative logistics solution involves installing smart kiosks at schools, universities, residential complexes, and corporate parks. These 24/7 self-service booths allow users to send mail anytime, solving the limited-hour constraint of traditional postal services in Canada. Users can choose from various mailing providers based on delivery speed and pricing, bringing efficiency and choice to everyday logistics.

- **Empire Furniture**: A home interior and furniture customization platform that lets users visualize and personalize their space. Customers can select furniture based on room size, color scheme, material, fabric, and design preferences. The platform even suggests matching pieces to create a cohesive aesthetic.

In summary, innovation can be applied in any industry or domain. By integrating intelligence, personalization, or efficiency into your business model, your idea could qualify for the Start-Up Visa. It's not about where you come from—it's about how forward-thinking your solution is.

What is the Cost or fee of Start Up Visa?

The total investment required for the Canada Start-Up Visa typically ranges between **CAD 100,000 to CAD 150,000 per family unit** (including husband, wife, and children). This amount covers a variety of critical services and deliverables essential for a successful application and business setup, including

- Fees for the designated **business incubator**
- **Office rental** expenses
- **Company incorporation** and business license fees
- **Legal fees** for filing Permanent Residency (PR) and Work Permit applications
- **CPA charges** for accounting, tax filing, and ongoing compliance
- **Consultant or legal services** for preparing and submitting Progress Reports at designated intervals
- **Compliance Report** preparation and submission services
- **Technical consulting** fees to develop a Minimum Viable Product (MVP) or a working prototype

(Note: Most incubators expect a product at Technology Readiness Level (TRL) 3–4, and IRCC may request a functional product during the review stage.)

Author's Insight

Choosing the right consultant for the Start-Up Visa program is absolutely critical. This process is highly complex and includes multiple deliverables, ranging from legal documentation to technical development and ongoing compliance. Your consultant must be experienced, knowledgeable, and well-versed in both the business and regulatory aspects of the Start-Up Visa.

As of **June 2024**, IRCC implemented major changes that have made the program significantly more competitive. Each designated organization, whether a business incubator, venture capitalist, or angel investor, is now limited to just **10 active slots**. This change has led to both a surge in demand and an increase in the fees charged by most Designated Organizations.

Unfortunately, many consultants have failed to obtain Work Permit approvals since these changes, largely due to **non-compliance with IRCC and CRA requirements** under the Start-Up Visa framework. However, between **May and July 2024**, I personally witnessed **26 Work Permit approvals** for projects handled by our team at *Migrant Master*. These approvals were not coincidental, they were the result of meticulous adherence to regulatory requirements and consistent performance in delivering quality progress.

I **strongly recommend** submitting the following reports **every quarter** to IRCC:

- Progress Report
- Compliance Report
- Technical Readiness Report

Regular submissions of these documents help IRCC assess the viability and authenticity of the business, which plays a vital role in securing both Work Permit and Permanent Residency approvals.

Chapter - 8

Real Estate Goldmine: Unlocking Guaranteed Returns in Canada

Canada's real estate market has long been one of the most stable and lucrative investment opportunities, attracting local and international investors alike. With a growing population, strong economic fundamentals, and high demand for housing and commercial properties, real estate in Canada offers a pathway to consistent returns, asset appreciation, and financial security.Canada's real estate market has demonstrated steady growth over the years, with property values appreciating in major cities such as Toronto, Vancouver, Montreal, and Calgary. The country's strong economy, coupled with low-interest mortgage options, makes real estate a safe and profitable investment. Even during economic downturns, property prices have shown resilience, making real estate an excellent choice for long-term wealth-building.

The residential sector remains a hot investment, with rental properties generating consistent passive income due to the high demand from students, immigrants, and working professionals. Condo developments, suburban housing, and short-term rentals through platforms like Airbnb offer excellent cash flow potential. Commercial real estate, including office spaces, retail properties, and industrial warehouses, provides high-yield investment opportunities. With the rise of e-commerce and business expansion, demand for commercial spaces continues to grow, making this sector particularly appealing to investors.

Why Invest in Under-Construction Properties?

Investing in under-construction properties is one of the smartest ways to maximize returns in Canada's real estate market. These properties offer several advantages, including significant price appreciation, flexible payment options, and delayed mortgage commitments, making them an attractive option for investors looking to secure profitable real estate deals.

Market Appreciation and Higher Returns

One of the biggest advantages of investing in under-construction properties is the potential for market appreciation. Since these properties are purchased at pre-launch or early development prices, their value tends to increase significantly by the time they are completed. With rising demand in major Canadian cities like Toronto and Vancouver, property values often appreciate by double-digit percentages before possession, allowing investors to build wealth quickly.

Flexible Payment Plans and Lower Initial Costs

Developers often offer structured and flexible payment plans that make investing in under-construction properties more affordable. Unlike fully built homes that require immediate full payment or mortgage approval, under-construction properties allow buyers to pay in phases. This reduces financial strain and enables investors to spread payments over several years, making real estate investment more accessible even for first-time buyers.

No Loan or Mortgage Payments Until Possession

Another key advantage is that investors are not required to start loan or mortgage payments until the property is completed. This allows buyers to secure prime real estate without the immediate burden of monthly mortgage payments, providing more time to arrange finances, build equity, or even resell the property at a higher price before closing. This delayed financial commitment makes under-construction properties a low-risk, high-reward investment strategy. Under-construction properties offer a cost-effective way to enter Canada's booming real estate market, providing strong appreciation potential, flexible payment structures, and financial breathing room before full ownership. For investors looking to maximize returns while minimizing upfront expenses, this strategy presents an ideal opportunity to secure valuable real estate at the best possible price.

Researching the Best Locations for Investment

Selecting the right location is crucial for maximizing returns in Canada's real estate market. High-growth areas with strong infrastructure, corporate expansion, and government-backed projects offer the best opportunities for long-term appreciation and rental demand. Identifying regions with rising property values and increasing demand ensures a profitable investment.

Upcoming Infrastructure Projects Driving Growth

Areas with new infrastructure developments, such as metro expansions, highways, and international airports, tend to experience rapid property appreciation. Improved connectivity attracts businesses, boosts tourism, and increases housing demand. Investors should focus on locations where major transit projects are planned, as these areas often witness skyrocketing real estate values over time.

Government and Corporate Developments Fueling Demand

Regions with government initiatives, economic incentives, and corporate expansions create stable investment opportunities. Cities with rising job markets due to new business headquarters, tech hubs, and manufacturing plants attract skilled workers, driving demand for residential and commercial properties. Areas benefiting from government-backed housing policies and tax incentives further enhance profitability for investors.

Emerging Neighborhoods in Growth Provinces

Certain provinces and cities have become prime real estate investment destinations due to their rapid urbanization and increasing population. Ontario remains the most sought-after province, with Toronto and its surrounding suburbs experiencing high appreciation due to growing job opportunities and strong rental demand. Expanding cities like Mississauga, Brampton, and Hamilton offer affordable alternatives with increasing property values. British Columbia continues to attract international investors, particularly in Vancouver and Surrey. The province's strong economy, natural beauty, and growing demand for housing make it a top choice for long-term real estate gains. Calgary has emerged as a high-growth market due to its affordable housing, strong job market, and economic diversification beyond oil and gas. The city's rising population and government initiatives have made it an attractive location for investors seeking properties with strong rental demand and appreciation potential.

Author's Insight: I have personally invested in real estate across Canada, primarily in Ontario, both for myself and on behalf of my clients. My focus has largely been on under-construction properties, and the returns have been remarkable. In many cases, these investments have yielded returns between CAD 100,000 to 150,000 within just two years.

Based on this experience, I strongly recommend investing in upcoming areas, particularly those near planned metro or subway stations or regions earmarked for significant infrastructure development. These zones often appreciate rapidly, offering investors both security and substantial capital growth potential.

Chapter - 9

Two Nations, Endless Possibilities: The India-Canada Connection

India and Canada share a deep and dynamic relationship, strengthened by shared democratic values, economic ties, and a thriving diaspora. The growing trade partnerships, cultural exchanges, and strong immigration links have created numerous opportunities for collaboration in business, education, and technology. Despite occasional political differences, both nations continue to foster bilateral trade, investment, and academic cooperation. Canada remains a top destination for Indian students, professionals, and entrepreneurs, contributing to the country's economy and multicultural society. With expanding business ties and a mutually beneficial economic relationship, the India-Canada connection is set to grow, offering endless possibilities for future partnerships and innovation.

A Resilient Bond

The relationship between India and Canada has faced occasional diplomatic challenges, particularly in the post-COVID era. While political tensions have surfaced at the governmental level, they have had little impact on the daily lives of Indians living in Canada. The strong Indian diaspora continues to thrive in business, education, and various professional fields, benefiting from Canada's inclusive and welcoming society. Instead of diplomatic hiccups, Canada remains a top destination for Indian immigrants, students, and entrepreneurs, reflecting the enduring strength of the bond between the two nations. The resilience of this relationship highlights the mutual benefits of collaboration and the potential for future growth in trade, investment, and cultural exchange.

Opportunities for Collaboration

The future of India-Canada relations is driven by shared economic interests, cultural ties, and innovation. Both nations have immense potential to strengthen their partnership across key sectors, fostering long-term growth and mutual prosperity.

Trade and Investment

India and Canada have a growing trade relationship, with expanding exports, imports, and investment flows. Canada's natural resources, energy sector, and agricultural exports complement India's manufacturing, IT, and service industries, creating significant business opportunities. Increased bilateral agreements and trade partnerships can further boost economic collaboration, benefiting businesses and entrepreneurs from both countries.

Education and Research

Canada is a top destination for Indian students, offering high-quality education, world-class research institutions, and post-graduation work opportunities. Universities in both countries continue to engage in collaborative research projects, particularly in technology, healthcare, and environmental sustainability. Strengthening academic ties can lead to joint research initiatives, student exchange programs, and skill development opportunities for future professionals.

Cultural Exchange

The Indian diaspora in Canada plays a crucial role in promoting cultural exchange through festivals, media, cuisine, and the arts. Bollywood, Indian literature, and traditional festivals like Diwali and Holi are widely celebrated across Canada, fostering cross-cultural understanding. Strengthening ties through film collaborations, art exhibitions, and cultural initiatives can further enhance people-to-people connections.

Healthcare and Technology

Both nations have thriving healthcare and technology sectors, presenting numerous opportunities for collaboration. India's pharmaceutical and biotech industries align well with Canada's medical research and innovation hubs, paving the way for advancements in vaccine development, AI-driven healthcare, and telemedicine solutions. Expanding tech partnerships in AI, cybersecurity, and digital transformation can drive economic growth and innovation in both countries. The India-Canada relationship holds immense potential for strategic collaboration across multiple sectors, paving the way for stronger trade, innovation, and cultural ties.

Section - B

Meet Our Experts: Trusted Professionals to Guide Your Immigration Journey

1. Consultant Secrets

Navigating the complexities of immigration can be challenging, but expert consultants play a crucial role in turning aspirations into reality. These professionals possess in-depth knowledge of visa programs, legal requirements, and application processes, ensuring smooth transitions for individuals and businesses looking to settle in Canada. From securing permanent residency through Express Entry and Start-Up Visa programs to guiding students, skilled professionals, and entrepreneurs, immigration consultants provide strategic insights and personalized solutions. Their expertise helps applicants avoid costly mistakes, streamline paperwork, and maximize their chances of approval. With an ever-changing immigration landscape, these trusted advisors empower clients with accurate guidance, helping them achieve their Canadian dream with confidence and clarity

Strategies for Client Success and Growth

Immigration agents, consultants, and lawyers play a vital role in helping individuals and businesses navigate Canada's immigration system effectively. Their success lies in tailored strategies, expert legal knowledge, and proactive problem-solving, ensuring a smooth transition for clients seeking permanent residency, work permits, or study visas. Experienced professionals emphasize the importance of personalized consultations, thorough documentation, and staying updated on policy changes. Strong client relationships, clear communication, and ethical practices are key to building trust and ensuring high approval rates. By leveraging digital tools, networking, and partnerships with global firms, immigration professionals continue to expand their reach, offering comprehensive solutions for students, skilled workers, and entrepreneurs looking to settle in Canada. Their insights and expertise drive client success and long-term business growth in an ever-evolving immigration landscape.

The Role of Immigration Agents in Securing Canadian Visas and Residency

Immigration agents serve as trusted advisors, guiding clients through the complexities of Canada's immigration system. Their expertise helps applicants identify the right programs, prepare strong applications, and navigate legal requirements with confidence. With years of experience handling visa applications, permanent residency processes, and work permits, these professionals offer strategic advice tailored to each client's background and goals. By staying up to date with policy changes and procedural updates, they ensure that clients have the best chance of success in securing their Canadian immigration status. Through personalized assessments and meticulous attention to detail, immigration agents simplify the process, making it more accessible and less stressful for individuals and families looking to start a new life in Canada.

Key Questions We Asked Immigration Experts

To gain deeper insights into the immigration process, we spoke with experienced agents and consultants about their strategies, challenges, and success stories in helping clients secure Canadian visas and permanent residency.

1. What strategies do you use to ensure a client's successful application?

Experts emphasize the importance of tailored guidance, thorough documentation, and proactive problem-solving. By carefully assessing each client's profile, they ensure applications meet eligibility criteria, reducing the risk of rejection. Keeping up with policy changes, leveraging strong legal knowledge, and providing step-by-step support are key to improving success rates.

2. What are some common challenges your clients face, and how do you help them overcome them?

Applicants often face issues such as incomplete paperwork, misinterpretation of immigration laws, and delays in processing. Consultants help clients by identifying red flags early, providing clear documentation checklists, and ensuring compliance with government requirements. Personalized consultations and legal expertise help clients navigate these obstacles with ease.

3. Can you share a success story where your intervention made all the difference for a client?

One consultant shared a case where a client's visa application had been previously denied due to missing financial documents. With expert intervention, the consultant restructured the application, gathered stronger supporting evidence, and submitted a compelling case. The client was eventually approved, securing permanent residency and successfully settling in Canada. By applying strategic solutions, personalized support, and deep legal expertise, immigration professionals transform challenges into success stories, helping clients achieve their Canadian dreams.

Education Transformers

India's education sector has undergone a remarkable transformation, with coaching centers playing a pivotal role in preparing students for global opportunities. These institutions serve as launchpads for academic and professional success, equipping students with the knowledge, skills, and confidence needed to excel in competitive exams and secure admissions to top universities abroad. With a focus on personalized mentorship, strategic learning methods, and industry-driven insights, India's leading coaching centers have become key drivers of student success. They bridge the gap between ambition and achievement, helping thousands of students navigate the complexities of international education. By providing expert guidance in entrance exams, language proficiency, and career counseling, these education pioneers continue to shape the future of India's youth, ensuring they thrive in global academic environments. Their commitment to excellence makes them true transformers of the education landscape, empowering students to achieve their dreams of studying and settling abroad.

The Hidden Heroes of Student Success

Behind every successful student who secures admission to a top international university, there are dedicated educators, mentors, and visionaries guiding them. The CEOs and founders of India's leading coaching centers play a crucial role in shaping students' futures by providing expert training, mentorship, and strategic preparation for competitive exams like IELTS, TOEFL, GRE, and GMAT. These education pioneers have built institutions that go beyond academics, fostering confidence, problem-solving skills, and global readiness in students. Their innovative teaching methodologies, data-driven strategies, and student-centric approaches have helped thousands achieve their dreams of studying abroad. Through insights from leading coaching center founders, we explore their journeys, the challenges they overcame, and the impact they've made in revolutionizing student success. Their contributions have transformed India's education landscape, making international opportunities more accessible than ever before.

The Transformative Role of Coaching Centers in India

Coaching centers in India have become a crucial bridge between education and global opportunities, shaping the futures of thousands of students. They go beyond traditional academics, providing specialized training for competitive exams, language proficiency, and career guidance to help students secure admissions in top international universities. As a key part of the immigration and education journey, these centers equip students with critical thinking skills, confidence, and cultural adaptability, ensuring they are well-prepared for academic success abroad. By offering personalized mentorship and expert guidance, they continue to play a transformative role in helping students achieve their dreams of studying and settling in global destinations like Canada, the U.S., and the U.K..

Inside the Minds of India's Leading Coaching Center Founders

This segment explores the journeys of the visionary CEOs and founders who have transformed India's coaching industry. These education leaders have built institutions that empower students with the skills, knowledge, and confidence needed to succeed in competitive exams and secure admissions abroad. By implementing innovative teaching strategies, personalized mentorship, and cutting-edge technology, they have revolutionized student learning and preparation. Their efforts have played a crucial role in helping aspiring students navigate the challenges of international education, particularly in countries like Canada, the U.S., and the U.K.

Through their commitment to excellence and student success, these pioneers continue to shape the future of global education, making overseas opportunities more accessible than ever before.

Key Questions We Asked Coaching Center Founders

1. What inspired you to start your coaching center, and what sets it apart from others?

Many coaching center founders were inspired by the growing demand for quality education and the need to guide students toward international opportunities. Their vision was to bridge the gap between ambition and achievement, ensuring that students from diverse backgrounds have access to world-class learning resources and expert mentorship.

2. How do you prepare students for international education through entrance exam coaching?

These coaching centers focus on comprehensive entrance exam preparation, equipping students with the necessary skills to excel in IELTS, TOEFL, GRE, GMAT, and other international tests. Through personalized study plans, structured practice sessions, and expert guidance, they help students build confidence, language proficiency, and test-taking strategies, making them ready for academic success abroad.

3. Can you share a memorable story where your coaching center played a pivotal role in a student's journey to success?

One founder shared the journey of a student who struggled with IELTS due to a lack of confidence in English. With consistent mentoring, customized learning techniques, and motivation, the student not only achieved a high IELTS score but also secured admission to a top university in Canada. Today, they are excelling in their studies, proving the transformative power of expert coaching and personalized guidance.

One Last Thing

If you found the book "**The Canadian Dream**" insightful and inspiring, We'd love to hear your thoughts! Whether it helped you understand new opportunities, navigate immigration pathways, or sparked fresh ideas for your journey, your feedback means the world to us.

Share your experiences, tell us how this book influenced your decisions, and let us know what resonated with you the most. Your stories and reviews help others see the possibilities ahead.

And if this book added value to your journey, don't forget to pass it along to friends, family, or anyone who could benefit from it. After all, great opportunities are even better when shared!

Please write to the Author

Dr. Swapnil Kale

skale@quickwin.in

Mobile: +91 9819221621